EVERYDAY
CAPE
MALAY
COOKING

EVERYDAY

CAPE
MALAY

COOKING

TEXT BY
ZAINAB LAGARDIEN
PHOTOGRAPHS BY
ALAIN PROUST

Struik Publishers (Pty) Ltd
(a member of Struik New Holland Publishing (Pty) Ltd)
Cornelis Struik House
80 McKenzie Street
Cape Town 8001

Reg. No.: 1954/000965/07

First published in hardcover in 1995
First published in softcover in 1998
4 6 8 10 9 7 5

EDITOR Glynne Williamson
DESIGNER Odette Marais
COVER DESIGN Odette Marais
PHOTOGRAPHER Alain Proust
STYLIST Macushla Falkiner
FOOD PREPARATION Ivy Tingwe and Zainab Lagardien

PROPS *Go East, Past Times, Hans Niehaus Collectors' Specialist,*
The Colonial Cotton Company, Collectors Corner Antiques,
The Junk Shop, Peter Visser Interiors, Stuttafords, Garlicks,
The Yellow Door, House & Interiors at Bric-a-Brac Lane

TYPESETTING Struik DTP
REPRODUCTION Hirt & Carter Cape (Pty) Ltd
PRINTING AND BINDING Craft (Pte.) Ltd, Singapore

ISBN 1 86825 696 0 (H/C)
ISBN 1 86872 168 X (S/C)

PUBLISHER'S NOTE
Please note that all cup measurements are approximate.

Contents

Acknowledgements

I dedicate this book to my son, Biejamien,
who becomes very noisy when he cooks
for a family wedding!

I wish to thank the Struik Publishing Group for accepting my manuscript and making a dream come true, especially director Linda de Villiers, designer Odette Marais and editor Glynne Williamson, who spent many hours in my kitchen learning our ways.

I also wish to give credit to photographer Alain Proust, stylist Macushla Falkiner and co-chef Ivy Tingwe for their professionalism.

I would also like to thank my family and friends for their support and encouragement in helping me compile this book, thereby preserving our traditions:

◎ My sister Fatima Abdul, also a caterer, for assisting with the catering ideas;

◎ My daughters (nee Solomon) Lutfeyah Jacobs, Mariam Tyers, Rashieda Isaacs and Noohr Samodien;

◎ My granddaughters Ruweyda Jacobs for copy typing, Shanaaz Tyers for typing all the fish dishes and Zyreena Tyers, my assistant who plays an important role in the catering;

◎ Nazley Gaidien for co-ordinating the typists, and to her daughters Shanaaz and Amina Gaidien;

◎ Fatima Du Preez, Mymoena Dollie and Rowlda Booley for also helping with the typing;

◎ Special thanks to my only son Bienjamien Solomon, a bulk cooker himself, for giving me moral support – with his wife, his four sisters and my granddaughters he could cater for and co-ordinate any large function;

◎ Lastly to my children's late father, Abdul Azeze Solomon, who inspired and encouraged me to put this book together.

Introduction

I was born (Bis'millah) at no. 14 Godfrey Street off Hanover Street in District Six. I was only six years old when my mother and the baby were laid to rest and I went to live with my grandmother. She was a well-known konfyt-maker, catering for special functions, and life with her was a very colourful one. She reared us on home-made breads and konfyts, so my sister and my introduction to cooking began at an early age!

First we learnt about fruit. To make konfyt, pieces of fig were nipped off in tiny spots, grated or cut with a cross at the bottom and lowered into salt water overnight. Oranges were done in the same way, with pips and pith removed. Then we learnt about fish. Snoek was salted and hung under a muslin cloth to dry in the wind. Before sunset it was strung up in the fireplace. Pounded snoek biltong with a pinch of fine chilli is still a family favourite, served with 'boeretroos' black coffee.

My grandmother made up for everything I'd lost in my mother, my aunts also helping with my culinary education. Aunty Fatima always iced the family biscuits, cakes and puddings, and also taught handicrafts. I was taught to decorate biscuits, then moved on to making quick smoortjies. Special lessons were given on

cooking and braising meats or making fish meals. Once I'd mastered these, my love for cooking, baking and brewing developed. The kitchen was, and still is, a busy place and the best place to be. Gradually my cooking and baking improved and I eventually went into bulk cooking for special occasions and to catering in hotels. By the time I left the hotel kitchens I'd become quite an expert – I'd enjoyed the challenges I'd put to myself and the experience has proved invaluable.

As I child I can remember breads being baked at the bakery for 2 pence a loaf. The bakery was opposite the wash-house where washing was done for 6 pence. Pickled snoek cost only 4 pence a piece (about 500 g folded double, ready to be steamed, flaked or smoored in a variety of ways). Mutton was sold for 6 pence a piece (about 500 g). Things have changed a bit since then!

Malay cooking can vary from tangy to moderately hot. The recipes in this book are not highly spiced and can be seasoned according to taste. Starseed petal (star anise) is the ingredient that I use to add a special flavour to many of my savoury dishes.

I hope that you and your family enjoy these recipes which have been gathered over many years and form part of our rich heritage. Insh'allah!

GLOSSARY

ALLSPICE
These are small, unripe, sun-dried berries of the pimento tree. The flavour is a combination of cinnamon, nutmeg and cloves and is used in curries, soups, bredies, desserts and cakes.

ANISEED
The seeds of the anise plant have a sweet, pungent flavour which is similar to liquorice, and are mainly used in confectionery.

ATJAR
Atjar is a relish made from sliced vegetables or fruit, flavoured with spices and covered with vinegar or oil.

BARISHAP
This is the Malay name for fennel seeds which have a slightly bitter aniseed flavour. Ground barishap is used in breyanis or fish dishes.

BAY LEAF
Bay leaves come from the evergreen bay or laurel tree and are used to flavour meat dishes, pickled fish, soups and bredies. They have a slightly bitter taste and must be discarded before the meal is served.

BOBOTIE
A favourite Malay dish, it is made of curried mince or fish baked slowly in the oven with a beaten egg poured over it. Bobotie is always served with rice.

BREDIE
A type of stew, the flavour is determined by the kind of vegetable added. Onions are browned in oil or fat, then meat (usually mutton or lamb) is added and braised over a low heat. Vegetables are added last and braised on top of the meat.

BREYANI
This is a semi-dry dish consisting of rice, spices and meat, chicken, fish, lentils or eggs, served in one pot.

CARDAMOM
Cardamom is a member of the ginger family, also known as the Seed of Paradise. It is sold ground or whole and is used to flavour curries, soups, eggs, salads, meat, breyanis, puddings and cakes.

CHILLI
Fresh chillies must be used sparingly, dried chilli more freely. Dried and powdered chillies are known as red or cayenne pepper. Green chillies have more flavour and are juicier, but the red chillies are hotter. Chillies are used to flavour curry dishes, chutneys and sambals.

CINNAMON
Cinnamon comes from the bark of a tropical tree which is rolled into cinnamon sticks or powdered. The lighter brown type is known as cinnamon. The reddish-brown cinnamon is called cassia. Cinnamon has a sweet flavour, a strong, spicy aroma and is used to flavour various drinks, savoury and sweet dishes.

CLOVES
Cloves are unopened buds of the myrtaceous tree which are picked when they turn red and then sun-dried. Ground cloves are stronger than whole ones. They are used as a pungent, fragrant

spice to flavour a variety of savoury and sweet dishes.

CURRY
Malay curry is slightly sweeter than Indian curry with less chilli and more spices. It is usually eaten with rice or rotis, accompanied by sambals.

CURRY LEAVES
These can be bought fresh or dried. Fresh ones are used to garnish curry meals. Dried ones add extra flavour to savoury dishes.

CURRY POWDER
A mixture of spices, it consists of cayenne pepper, coriander, cumin seed, fenugreek, turmeric, cinnamon, cardamom, cloves, fennel, ginger, mace, mustard and black or white pepper.

DHAL
Dhal is an Indian lentil often used in breyanis.

DHANIA
Fresh coriander leaves, or dhania, are used to garnish curries or to add flavour to savoury dishes. It is also available in powdered form.

EID
Two Eids are celebrated during the year – Eidul-Fitr (the Festival of Charity) and Eidul-Adgha (the Festival of Sacrifice). Eidul-Fitr takes place the day after Ramadan and is often referred to as Labarang. Eidul-Adgha takes place 70 days after Ramadan.

GARLIC
This is a bulbous plant, smaller than an onion, with a strong taste. It can be used fresh or dried to flavour savoury dishes and is often used along with fresh root ginger.

This is a mixture of certain spices, used in breyanis, curries, atjars and other savoury dishes. There are many different varities of masala, including red leaf (which contains more ground chilli powder), leaf and tandoori masala.

KABOB
A kabob is a hard-boiled egg wrapped in mince meat and fried in fat or oil.

LABARANG
Refer to entry under 'Eid'.

METHI
Methi, or fenugreek, is the pod of an annual plant related to the pea. The seed is finely ground and mixed with curry powder to flavour rice, atjars and vegetable dishes.

MINT
Mint is a fresh tasting herb with a strong flavour which must be used sparingly.

MUSTARD SEED
This is a small, dark seed used to flavour atjars, pickles and savoury dishes.

NAARTJIE PEEL
Naartjie peel is dried, ground into a powder and stored in a jar to flavour cakes, puddings, meat dishes and vegetables. It goes well with cardamom and cinnamon.

NUTMEG
Nutmeg comes from the seeds of the fruit of an evergreen treeThe dried membrane that surrounds the fruit is mace. Nutmeg is used to flavour bredies and confectionery.

PEPPER
Black and white pepper comes from a vine which bears small berries. When picked just before ripe, they yield black pepper. Ripe berries are sun-dried and ground to form white pepper.

ROSEWATER
The essence from rose petals is used to flavour puddings and milk drinks.

RAMADAN
This is the ninth month of the Muslim year during which strict fasting occurs, starting before sunrise and ending at sunset. This most important of all fasts ends after 30 days when the new moon has been sighted.

ROTI
Roti is the Malay word for unleavened bread adapted from the Indian recipe. It is often served unbuttered with certain curries instead of rice, the roti scooping up the curry in place of cutlery.

SAFFRON
Saffron is a rare and expensive spice made from the stamens of the wild crocus and used to tint and flavour savoury dishes.

SAMBAL
Of Javanese origin, a sambal is a tangy condiment, made from grated vegetables or fruit, salted and flavoured with vinegar and chillies. It is usually served with curries or bredies.

SMOOR
Smoor can be translated to mean braised. Vegetables and meat can be smoored together in oil or fat.

STARSEED PETAL
This is also called star anise because of its star shape. The seeds have a tangy flavour and are used whole or ground in savoury dishes.

TAMARIND
This is the fruit of a tropical tree with a sweetish-sour flavour. The fruit is boiled or is sometimes sucked raw for the taste. The pods are pulped, boiling water is poured over a lump of tamarind and left to soak for a short while, resulting in tamarind water. This liquid is used to flavour curries.

TURMERIC
Turmeric comes from a perennial tropical plant and is a member of the ginger family. The root is dried and ground and used to colour curry and rice and flavour savoury dishes. It is sometimes called 'borrie'.

Soups and Light Meals

Soups, nourishing and tasty, are a popular winter's meal and are often served during the fast of Ramadan. Some of the light meals can also be served as snacks or as accompaniments to a delicious feast!

Split Pea and Dumpling Soup

Subtly spiced pea soup with dumplings make a filling lunch-time meal.

½ kg stewing beef
2 pieces sheep shin
1 medium onion, chopped
about 2 litres (8 cups) boiling water
500 g (2½ cups) dried split peas, soaked overnight in boiling water
10 ml (2 tsp) medium-coarse salt
1 tomato, blanched, peeled and pulped
3 young carrots, scraped
2 large potatoes, peeled and halved
10 ml (2 tsp) tomato paste
3 whole cloves
4 allspice
1 starseed petal (star anise)
5 ml (1 tsp) white sugar
125 ml (½ cup) chopped parsley
125 ml (½ cup) chopped celery

DUMPLINGS
250 ml (1 cup) self-raising flour
10 ml (2 tsp) melted butter
a pinch ground nutmeg

IN A DEEP POT on medium heat scorch the meat and onion. Pour the boiling water onto the meat and add remaining soup ingredients, except parsley and celery. Cook soup for about 50 minutes. Remove carrots and potatoes, mash them and return to the pot. Reduce heat and add parsley and celery.

Make a thick dough by mixing the flour, butter and nutmeg with a little liquid from the soup. Dipping a dessertspoon into the pot and then into the dough prevents the dough sticking to the spoon. Drop spoonfuls of dough into the soup to make dumplings. After 10 minutes remove from heat and serve. SERVES 6

Masala Fried Snoek Roe

500 ml (2 cups) oil
1 kg snoek roe, washed and dried
5 ml (1 tsp) salt
5 ml (1 tsp) red masala
2 cardamom pods, lightly crushed

HEAT OIL IN a saucepan over medium heat. While oil is heating, marinate roe with salt and masala. Add cardamom pods to the oil. Slice roe and add, taking care not to crowd the saucepan. After 5 minutes, reduce heat to low. Continue until all the roes are cooked and golden-brown. Drain roes, reserving oil, and serve with chips. SERVES 8

OPPOSITE   Old Cape Cream of Tomato Soup, page 12

Old Cape Cream of Tomato Soup

This recipe won me first prize in a Cape Argus cookery competition a few years ago.

500 g fresh ripe tomatoes
175 ml (³/4 cup) red lentils
1 kg sheep knuckles
3 marrow bones
1 medium onion, finely chopped
3 litres (12 cups) boiling water
1 large turnip *or* potato,
peeled and cubed
4 medium carrots, peeled
and cubed
15 ml (1 tbsp) tomato paste
5 allspice
5 whole cloves
10 ml (2 tsp) sugar
125 ml (¹/2 cup) chopped parsley
125 ml (¹/2 cup) chopped celery
5 ml (1 tsp) black or white pepper
a pinch turmeric
fresh cream for serving

BLANCH TOMATOES, PEEL and chop. Soak lentils in lukewarm water for about 30 minutes and set aside. Soak meat and bones in lukewarm water for about 5 minutes and set aside. Rinse meat and bones twice.

Heat a deep, heavy-based cooking pot on medium heat. Transfer meat and bones to pot and top with onion. Scorch meat slightly but do not braise. Add 2 litres (8 cups) of boiling water and leave to cook for about 1¹/2 hours, stirring occasionally. Add turnip or potato and carrots and the rest of ingredients except parsley, celery, pepper and turmeric. Cook for about 30 minutes.

During the cooking process, remove any scum that may form on the surface. Add parsley and celery and cook slowly for 30 minutes before serving time. Add pepper and turmeric and stir well. Serve with a tablespoon of cream swirled into each bowl. SERVES 8

Barley Soup

A favourite, well-tried soup with an added tang of starseed petal.

500 g neck of mutton
2 marrow bones
500 g mutton knuckles
375 ml (1¹/2 cups) barley
1 onion, chopped
3 litres (12 cups) boiling water
3 carrots, peeled and cubed
1 turnip *or* potato, peeled and cubed
and soaked in cold water
2 soft, red tomatoes,
blanched, peeled and pulped
6 allspice
4 whole cloves
1 starseed petal (star anise)
15 ml (1 tbsp) salt
15 ml (1 tbsp) tomato paste
5 ml (1 tsp) white pepper
125 ml (¹/2 cup) chopped parsley
125 ml (¹/2 cup) chopped celery

SOAK MEAT FOR about 5 minutes and barley for about 1 hour separately in lukewarm water. Drain meat. Heat a saucepan on medium heat and add meat and onion. Allow to scorch a little. Pour over 1 litre (4 cups) boiling water and raise temperature to high. Add the remaining 2 litres (8 cups) boiling water.

Drain barley and add to saucepan with remaining ingredients except pepper, parsley and celery. Cook rapidly for 1 hour, removing any scum that may form but taking care not to discard the spices. Reduce heat to low and add remaining ingredients. Simmer for a further 30 minutes. SERVES 6

Farm-Style Soup

Chunky and hearty, this soup is perfect for a cold winter's night!

15 ml (1 tbsp) oil
3 slices beef shin
2 marrow bones *or* 1 kg mutton
knuckles
1 medium onion, chopped
3 litres (12 cups) boiling water
4 young carrots, peeled and cubed
500 g tomatoes, blanched and peeled
1 x 410 g tin whole-kernel corn
¹/2 small spitskop cabbage
(curly top), finely grated
4 whole cloves
6 allspice
15 ml (1 tbsp) tomato paste
10 ml (2 tsp) sugar
10 ml (2 tsp) salt
2,5 ml (¹/2 tsp) turmeric
1 x 410 g tin baked beans
125 ml (¹/2 cup) chopped parsley
125 ml (¹/2 cup) chopped celery
10 ml (2 tsp) ground black pepper

THIS SOUP WILL take 2 hours to cook in a saucepan or 20 minutes in a pressure cooker.

Heat oil in a saucepan and scorch meat and onions but do not braise. Add 2 litres (8 cups) boiling water to saucepan. Add the remaining ingredients, except baked beans, celery, parsley and pepper, and cook rapidly for 2 hours, removing any scum that may form. Return to the saucepan any spices that were scooped up in the process. Now add 1 litre (4 cups) boiling water and turn heat to low.

Add remaining ingredients, except beans, and simmer until meat is tender and vegetables are cooked. Add the beans 5 minutes before serving. SERVES 6

N O T E S

✔ The flavour of soup is not complete without adding marrow bones to the soup during cooking.

Country-Style Bunny Chow

Baked Bean Soup

500 g stewing beef, cubed
2 marrow bones
1 medium onion, chopped
2 litres (8 cups) boiling water
20 ml (1¹/₂ tbsp) tomato paste
1 small tomato, blanched, peeled and chopped
1 turnip *or* potato, peeled and diced
4 medium carrots, peeled and diced
60 ml (¹/₄ cup) chopped celery
1 starseed petal (star anise)
5 allspice
5 whole cloves
1 x 410 g tin baked beans
5 ml (1 tsp) pepper
60 ml (¹/₄ cup) chopped parsley

HEAT A SAUCEPAN on medium heat and add meat and marrow bones. Add the chopped onion to the meat and scorch until it is lightly browned – do not allow to braise. Now add boiling water and remaining ingredients except baked beans, pepper and parsley. Cook for about 40 minutes. Remove any scum that may form on the surface, taking care not to discard the spices. Add baked beans, pepper and parsley 10 minutes before serving. SERVES 4-5

Country-Style Bunny Chow

The 'Bunny' represents the loaf, supposedly the size of a rabbit, and 'Chow' is a Durban-Indian word for filling.

CHOW
15 ml (1 tbsp) oil
1 onion, chopped
250 g tenderized steak, cubed
250 ml (1 cup) water
2,5 ml (¹/₂ tsp) turmeric
2,5 ml (¹/₂ tsp) masala
2,5 ml (¹/₂ tsp) salt
1 piece stick cinnamon
10 ml (2 tsp) tomato sauce
2,5 ml (¹/₂ tsp) garlic and ginger paste
2,5 ml (¹/₂ tsp) ground jeera (cumin)
3 slices red pepper
1 x 410 g tin butter beans, drained

BUNNY
2 small, oval loaves *or* short French loaves

HEAT OIL OVER medium heat, add onion and scorch. Add steak and water, steam until the water has cooked away, then stir-fry until meat is just tender. Add remaining ingredients, taking care to add the beans last. Slice off a quarter of the loaf lengthwise, scoop out some of the bread and fill with the chow. No cutlery needed here! SERVES 2

Dhaltjies

The Malay word for chilli bites is dhaltjies.

375 ml (1½ cups) pea flour or
Chilli Bite Mix
175 ml (¾ cup) self-raising flour
½ bunch spinach leaves,
torn into small pieces
5 ml (1 tsp) salt
5 ml (1 tsp) turmeric
2,5 ml (½ tsp) red masala
60 g (¼ cup) fresh ginger
1 green chilli, chopped *or*
2,5 ml (½ tsp) crushed chillies
1 small onion, finely chopped
1 slice red pepper, finely chopped
5 ml (1 tsp) ground jeera (cumin)
30 ml (2 tbsp) butter, melted
5 ml (1 tsp) baking powder
about 250 ml (1 cup) water
375 ml (1½ cups) oil for deep-frying

MIX ALL THE INGREDIENTS together, except for the oil, to make a fairly stiff batter – it must be manageable but not runny.

Heat oil in a deep pan on medium heat until warm but not hot. Dip a dessertspoon into the oil, then into the mixture (this prevents the batter from sticking to the spoon), and drop spoonfuls of batter into the oil. Fry slowly until golden-brown and crisp. Make sure that the oil doesn't get too hot during frying.

Pierce with a fork to test if they are cooked – if the fork is dry, the dhaltjies are ready. Remove from pan and allow to drain on kitchen paper or in a colander.

Serve immediately as a snack or starter. MAKES ABOUT 30, DEPENDING ON SIZE

N O T E S

✔ Dhaltjies can be frozen if dried chillis have been used. Freeze wrapped in foil or in an airtight container.
✔ If using Chilli Bite Mix, test batter before adding salt as it contains salt already.

Samoosas

Of Indian origin, these piquant pastry triangles are time-consuming to make but the results are worth the effort. Samoosa pastry is known as pur.

4 x 250 ml (4 cups) cake flour
5 ml (1 tsp) turmeric
5 ml (1 tsp) salt
375 ml (1½ cup) lukewarm water
10 ml (2 tsp) oil
500 g steak mince
2,5 ml (½ tsp) cayenne pepper
1 green chilli or a pinch cayenne pepper
a pinch jeera (cumin) seeds
a pinch leaf masala
1 medium onion, chopped
oil for deep-frying

FORM A SOFT dough with the flour, a pinch turmeric, salt and water. Leave to stand.

Heat oil in a saucepan. Stir-fry meat with all remaining ingredients except onion. Stir until dry and remove from heat.

Pour a little boiling water on onion, leave for a few minutes and strain. Spoon into a clean cloth and twist cloth tightly to extract excess liquid and strong flavour of onion. Add to meat and mix well. The filling must be dryish or it will escape from the pastry during cooking.

Sprinkle a little flour onto a table or board. Break off balls of dough, the size of eggs – keep hands and rolling pin well-floured and roll out four of the balls as thin as possible into four circles. Smear the dough circles with a little oil, especially the edges. Lightly sprinkle some flour round the edges and middle. Repeat the process until you have a stack of four circles. Do not oil the top or the bottom circle. Roll out the stacked circles into one large, thin circle and cut the sides evenly to form a square.

Place pastry on an ungreased baking sheet or roti griddle. Parbake at 100 °C for 2-3 minutes. When leaves show signs of loosening, remove from the baking sheet. With a sharp knife, cut into 14 cm x 6 cm strips. Separate layers. Cover with a damp cloth to prevent the pastry from drying out.

Hold a strip of pastry in one hand and pull the bottom corner across. Fold upwards to form a triangle with sharp corners and a pocket and fill with the mince mixture. Fold the pastry across the top of the triangle to seal. Make a thick paste with 60 ml (¼ cup) flour and a little cold water. Use this paste to stick ends together after filling. The filling will escape during cooking if the samoosa is not folded down well.

Deep-fry in hot oil over medium heat, turning once or twice until golden-brown. Remove from pan with a slotted spoon and drain on absorbent paper. MAKES ABOUT 24 SAMOOSAS

N O T E S

✔ Samoosas can be frozen but for no longer than 6 months and can be deep-fried immediately without defrosting.
✔ The leftover pur can be deep-fried slowly in hot oil.

Fish Cakes

A favourite weekday meal that's quick and economical to make.

1 x 410 g tin middlecut *or*
extra-large plain pilchards
1 small onion
4 cloves garlic
60 ml (¼ cup) parsley *or*
6 mint leaves, chopped
4 slices stale white bread, soaked in
water for 5 minutes and squeezed dry
a pinch turmeric
a pinch grated nutmeg
1 egg, lightly beaten
5 ml (1 tsp) butter
a pinch salt
1 green pepper, chopped
oil for frying

DRAIN FISH, REMOVE centre bones and place in a mixing bowl. Chop onion, garlic and parsley separately – the parsley should be finer than the onion and the garlic much finer than the parsley – and add to the fish. Add the bread and mix together.

Add the remaining ingredients and mix lightly. Wet your hands in a small bowl of cold water before forming small round fish cakes. Fry in not-too-deep oil over medium heat. For crispy fish cakes, turn a colander upside-down over the pan while frying.

Serve with cooked white rice, adding 2 small pieces of stick cinnamon and a pinch turmeric for extra flavour and colour. Chutney on the side rounds off the meal. SERVES 5

Snoek Roe Smoortjie

Serve with fresh rolls as a light lunch.

60 ml (¼ cup) oil drained from
Masala Fried Snoek Roe (page 10)
1 small onion, chopped
3 tomatoes, blanched, peeled
and pulped
a pinch salt
10 ml (2 tsp) sugar

6 slices red *or* green pepper
6 snoek roes, washed and
slightly dried

HEAT OIL IN a saucepan, toss in onion and braise until golden-brown. Add tomato. Keep heat on medium and braise onion and tomato. Now add salt, sugar and sliced pepper.

Cut roes into portions, add to the saucepan and simmer for 10 minutes. Serve immediately. SERVES 5

Pickled Kabeljou

Pickled fish is traditionally served over the festive season.

1 medium kabeljou, sliced
15 ml (1 tbsp) salt
10 ml (2 tsp) red leaf masala
185 ml (¾ cup) oil
2 cardamom pods, split open
375 ml (1½ cups) malt vinegar

10 ml (2 tsp) turmeric
15 ml (1 tbsp) sugar
2 medium onions, sliced into rings
250 ml (1 cup) water
1 bay leaf
4 allspice
1 whole clove

WASH FISH AND marinate in 5 ml (1 tsp) salt and 2,5 ml (½ tsp) masala for about 2 minutes. Heat pan, add oil and cardamom and fry fish in shallow oil until light brown. Spread fish in large, shallow dish. Set aside.

Heat saucepan and add vinegar, turmeric, sugar, remaining salt and masala, onion rings and water. Bring to boil and remove from heat.

Toss in bay leaf and spices, cover and leave to cool slightly. When lukewarm, pour mixture over fish ensuring that fish is completely covered. For the best results, store, covered, in a glass dish for 24 hours to allow the flavours to develop. SERVES 4

Pickled Kabeljou

Fish and Seafood

The Cape Malays have had fishermen in their families for generations, and fish, served in a variety of dishes, has become a favourite item on the menu. Snoek is particularly popular and is prepared in almost any way imagineable!

Old Cape Smoorsnoek

Smoorsnoek is popular amongst the Malay community – this is one of my favourite versions.

60 ml (¼ cup) oil
1 onion, chopped
500 g salted, dried snoek,
steamed and shredded
5 ml (1 tsp) sugar
1 red *or* green chilli, chopped
1 x 410 g tin peas *or*
410 g frozen peas

HEAT OIL IN a broad, shallow saucepan, toss in chopped onion and braise. Add steamed and shredded snoek, sugar, chilli and peas. Reduce heat to low for 5 minutes, then remove from heat and serve with white rice and Apricot and Peach Chutney (page 63). SERVES 4

Oven Snoek

The ingredients used in this traditional Malay fish dish enhance the special flavour of the snoek.

1 medium, freshly caught snoek
10 ml (2 tsp) coarse salt
5 ml (1 tsp) red masala
45 ml (3 tbsp) melted butter *or* margarine
a few tomato slices
a few onion rings

REMOVE THE HEAD and tail of the fish and set these pieces aside. Wash remainder of fish well and salt. Cut the side bone to allow the salt to soak into the fish, leave to stand for a few minutes, then dust with masala.
Preheat the oven to 200 °C. Grease a roasting pan lightly with a little of the butter. Place fish on pan and top with the remaining butter, the tomato slices and onion rings. Bake the snoek for about 25 minutes or until the fish is cooked.
Serve with Light Brown Rolls (page 90) and Chilli Sauce (page 65) or Apricot and Peach Chutney (page 63). SERVES 6

NOTES

✔ Instead of using peas in the Old Cape Smoorsnoek recipe, add a shredded spitskop (curly top) cabbage and a pinch of turmeric.
✔ Make a smoor with the head and tail of the fish from Oven Snoek by steaming with salt, onion and ground black pepper. Alternatively, use the Old Cape Smoorsnoek recipe on this page.

OPPOSITE   Oven Snoek

Crispy Silverfish

The silverfish is a soft, moist and tasty fish and is flavoured here with garlic, turmeric and masala.

2 small, freshly caught silverfish,
scaled and gutted
10 ml (2 tsp) salt
5 ml (1 tsp) turmeric
5 ml (1 tsp) roasted red masala
3 cloves garlic, crushed
125 ml (½ cup) oil
60 ml (¼ cup) flour for coating

MIX SPICES TOGETHER and marinate fish for a few minutes in a glass or porcelain dish.

Heat oil in a heavy-based pan over medium heat. Coat fish lightly with flour and transfer to pan. Fry each side until done. Serve on a platter with Long-Grain White Rice (page 54). Stir-fried onions and Braised Tomato (page 52) are good accompaniments. SERVES 3

Tangy Pilchard Smoor

An economical, weekday meal.

60 ml (¼ cup) oil
3 pieces stick cinnamon
1 large onion, chopped
15 ml (1 tbsp) tomato sauce
250 ml (1 cup) water
a pinch turmeric
5 ml (1 tsp) leaf masala
8 curry leaves
a pinch salt
a pinch sugar
1 starseed petal (star anise)
1 x 410 g can plain pilchards, drained
and middle bone removed

HEAT OIL AND cinnamon in a saucepan. Add onion and braise lightly. Add remaining ingredients, cover saucepan and cook for a few minutes to allow the flavour to develop. Turn off heat.

It is now ready to serve with white rice. SERVES 5

Kabeljou Tomato Smoor

The kabeljou (named from the Dutch 'kabeljauw') is complemented by the tomato smoor.

1 small kabeljou, sliced
375 ml (1½ cups) oil
10 ml (2 tsp) cake flour

MARINADE
10 ml (2 tbsp) salt
3,5 ml (½ tsp) leaf masala
4 cloves garlic, crushed

SMOOR
30 ml (2 tbsp) oil
1 medium onion,
thinly sliced
250 g (1 cup) tomatoes, diced
2,5 ml (½ tsp) salt
10 ml (2 tsp) sugar
3 slices green pepper
a pinch masala

WASH AND DRAIN fish. Mix the marinade ingredients together and rub into the fish. Leave to marinate for a few minutes.

To make the smoor, heat the oil in a pan, add onion and braise until lightly browned. Add tomato, salt, sugar and sliced pepper and cook for 10 minutes over low heat. Remove from heat and add masala. Set aside and keep warm.

Heat oil in a heavy-based pan on medium-high. Dust fish lightly on both sides with flour and place in pan. (Dusting the fish with flour prevents the flesh from breaking up and also gives it a golden colour.) Cover with lid and cook, turning when golden-brown.

Serve the fish and tomato smoor with Savoury Rice (page 54). SERVES 5

N O T E

✔ Use Hottentot instead of kabeljou.

Fish Bobotie

A simply delicious dish! Any type of firm white fish can be used.

500 g hake steaks
10 ml (2 tsp) chopped parsley
6 fresh mint leaves, chopped
3 cloves garlic, crushed
10 ml (2 tsp) soft margarine
a pinch leaf masala
5 ml (1 tsp) salt
a pinch grated nutmeg
a pinch ground black pepper
1 small tomato, cubed
a pinch turmeric
1 small onion, chopped
4 slices stale bread, soaked in
water for 5 minutes
2 eggs, lightly beaten

STEAM FISH IN a little water over medium heat for 10 minutes. Remove from heat and allow to cool. Flake fish and set aside.

Mix remaining ingredients, except the 2 lightly beaten eggs, adding bread last. Do not squeeze all the water out of the bread otherwise the mixture will be too stiff. Add the fish to this mixture.

Bake in the oven at 200 °C until light brown and remove from oven. Pour the beaten eggs over the fish mixture and return to the oven for a further 10 minutes or until it is browned on top.

Serve immediately with chutney, Cinnamon Pumpkin (page 52) and mashed potatoes. SERVES 4

Cape Salmon Smoor

If Cape salmon is unavailable, use soldaat (santa) instead.

1,5 kg Cape Salmon cutlets
7,5 ml (1½ tsp) salt
5 ml (1 tsp) leaf masala
250 ml (1 cup) oil
1 large onion, chopped
1 small tomato, blanched, peeled
and pulped

Fish Bobotie, page 18, served with Cinnamon Pumpkin, page 52

4 potatoes, peeled and cubed
500 ml (2 cups) water
10 ml (2 tsp) salt
1/2 red *or* green pepper, sliced
1 small green chilli, halved
1 starseed petal (star anise)

MIX 7,5 ML SALT (1 1/2 tsp) and masala together, rub into the fish and allow to marinate for 10 minutes. Heat 125 ml (1/2 cup) oil in a pan and fry fish lightly for 5 minutes each side. Remove from pan and set aside.

Use the same pan and the remaining 125 ml (1/2 cup) oil to make the smoor. Heat the oil on medium heat and when warm, but not too hot, toss in the onion and braise until golden-brown. Stir occasionally.

Now add the tomato and potatoes with 375 ml (1 1/2 cups) cold water and 2,5 ml (1/2 tsp) salt. Cook for about 10 minutes.

Reduce heat and add fish and remaining ingredients. Add the remaining 125 ml (1/2 cup) cold water and simmer gently. When done, serve with Braised Brown Rice (page 54) and Chilli Sauce (page 65). SERVES 5

Masala Stumpnose

Kingklip, Cape salmon or snoek can be substituted for the stumpnose in this piquant dish.

1,5 kg white stumpnose
10 ml (2 tsp) salt
1 clove garlic, chopped
1 green chilli *or*
2,5 ml (1/2 tsp) cayenne pepper
5 ml (1 tsp) leaf masala
5 ml (1 tsp) turmeric
1 lemon
375 ml (1 1/2 cups) oil
2 cardamom pods, split open

REMOVE FINS FROM fish and cut fish into portions. Slit each portion at the top and salt the fish – the slits must be wide enough for the salt to soak in. Mix garlic, chilli, masala and turmeric together, then rub into fish and allow to marinate for a few minutes. Watch out for sharp bones while marinating!

Halve the lemon, remove the pips and squeeze the juice over the fish portions. Heat oil and the crushed cardamom on medium heat and fry fish, covered.

Serve with Long-Grain White Rice (page 54) and Cabbage, Carrot and Bean Atjar (page 62). SERVES 6

N O T E

✔ Fish scales can easily be removed after soaking the fish in cold water for a while.

Smoorvis and Butter Beans

Instead of soaking beans overnight, using tinned butter beans makes this a quick dish to prepare.

half a salted snoek
60 ml (¼ cup) oil
1 onion, sliced
1 small tomato, blanched, peeled and pulped
5 ml (1 tsp) leaf masala
a pinch turmeric
1 cardamom pod
2 pieces stick cinnamon
a pinch ground jeera (cumin)
a pinch coriander
2 x 410 g tins butter beans, drained

SOAK SNOEK IN cold water overnight. Rinse and steam in very little water. If you are in a hurry and don't have time for overnight soaking, pour a kettle of boiling water over the snoek, rinse and leave for a few minutes in a little cold water. Bone and flake the fish, the set aside.

Heat oil in a saucepan and braise onion until golden-brown. Add tomato and cook for a few minutes. Now mix fish, then add spices just before fish is cooked. Simmer for a further 15 minutes before adding butter beans. Allow to heat through and serve with Long-Grain White Rice (page 54). SERVES 4

Shrimp-á-la-Taiwan

Shrimps are an extravagance but worth it.

125 ml (½ cup) oil
4 small pieces stick cinnamon
2 cardamom pods
1 large onion, chopped
1 small tomato, blanched, peeled and pulped
15 ml (1 tbsp) tomato sauce
2 x 454 g packets peeled shrimps
5 ml (1 tsp) turmeric
5 ml (1 tsp) masala
12 curry leaves
¼ red *or* green pepper, chopped
5 ml (1 tsp) garlic and ginger paste
1 starseed petal (star anise)
7,5 ml (1½ tsp) salt
6 allspice
2 whole cloves
60 g (¼ cup) tamarind, soaked for 5 minutes in 125 ml (½ cup) boiling water with 5 ml (1 tsp) sugar
5 ml (1 tsp) ground jeera (cumin)

HEAT OIL IN a heavy-based saucepan over medium heat. Add cinnamon and cardamom, then onion, and braise until golden-brown. Add tomato and tomato sauce and stir to mix thoroughly.

Cook shrimps according to packet instructions. Add shrimps and the remaining ingredients to the onion mixture, except tamarind and jeera. Reduce heat.

Strain the tamarind through a sieve and, with the jeera, add the liquid to the mixture. Simmer gently for 5 minutes, stirring once or twice.

Serve with Long-Grain White Rice (page 54). SERVES 6

NOTE

✔ Make sure that you always buy fresh fish with bright, bulging eyes – never buy fish with dull eyes.

Trawler's Favourite Pangha

Pangha are firm, pinkish fish which are trawled all year round.

2 medium panghas
10 ml (2 tsp) salt
5 ml (1 tsp) leaf masala
4 cloves garlic, crushed
1 lemon, halved, pips removed
1 small green chilli, chopped
1 large onion, sliced
375 ml (1½ cups) oil
4 ripe tomatoes, cubed
1 starseed petal (star anise)
½ red *or* green pepper, sliced
10 ml (2 tsp) sugar
2 cardamom pods, split open

CLEAN AND DIVIDE fish into cutlets. As panghas' bones are very hard, chop off as much as possible. Wash cutlets under slow-running cold water, then drain well. Mix 7,5 ml (1½ tsp) of the salt, the masala and garlic together. Add juice of half the lemon and chopped chilli. Pour over cutlets and allow to marinate for a few minutes.

Braise onion in 15 ml (1 tbsp) of the oil in a light pan. Add tomatoes, the remaining salt, starseed, pepper slices and sugar. Reduce heat and cook for 10 minutes.

If tomatoes are very watery, cook a little longer, but don't let the mixture become too dry. Reduce heat to medium and fry fish in the remaining oil. Add one of the cardamom pods to the oil while frying the first batch of cutlets, and the other while frying the second batch.

Enjoy this dish with Long-Grain White Rice (page 54) and tomato sauce or Chilli Sauce (page 65). SERVES 6

BELOW   Khitchri Rice, page 54, and Smoorvis and Butter Beans, page 20

Poultry

The Muslims do not eat pork, so poultry, meat and fish form part of their daily diet. Chicken and turkey dishes are often served during the Feast of Labarang (the Festival of Charity) while some are simply for everyday enjoyment.

Chicken Pie

The masala and cinnamon liven up an otherwise ordinary chicken pie. Serve with mashed potato and salads or vegetables.

FILLING
7,5 ml (1½ tsp) salt
5 ml (1 tsp) red masala
2 chicken drumsticks, deboned and each divided into three
2 chicken breasts, deboned and each divided into three
5 ml (1 tsp) margarine
2 small pieces stick cinnamon
15 ml (1 tbsp) oil *or*
10 ml (2 tsp) butter
1 small onion, chopped
4 small shreds green *or* red pepper
5 ml (1 tsp) red masala
2,5 ml (½ tsp) dried thyme
10 ml (2 tsp) cornflour made into paste with water and a pinch salt

PASTRY
310 ml (1¼ cups) cake flour
125 ml (½ cup) self-raising flour
125 g (½ cup) butter
250 ml (1 cup) cold water
15 ml (1 tbsp) lemon juice
10 ml (2 tsp) oil
2,5 ml (½ tsp) salt
1 egg, beaten

MIX SALT AND masala together, rub into chicken pieces, and allow to marinate for a few minutes. Grill in a heavy-based saucepan in margarine on medium heat. Add cinnamon and small quantities of water as the meat grills. Remove from heat when cooked and set aside to cool.

Heat oil or butter in a pan and stir-fry onion and pepper shreds. Add remaining filling ingredients except cornflour paste. When heated through, slowly stir in cornflour paste for a few minutes. Remove from heat. To make the pastry, sift flours together and lightly rub in butter. Adding water a little at a time, add remaining ingredients, except egg, and form into a dough.

Rest dough for 15 minutes, roll out and divide in half. Line a round, oven-proof dish with half the pastry and bake blind for 5 minutes on middle shelf at 200 °C. Remove from oven and leave to cool.

Spoon in the filling evenly. Place other half of pastry on top, press down and seal overhanging edge. Cut off excess pastry, crimp edges with a pastry cutter, and prick top with a fork. Brush with beaten egg before and after baking. Return to oven and bake for 30 minutes. SERVES 4

OPPOSITE   Malayan Crumbed Chicken, page 24

Javanese Chicken

My ancestors come from Java and this delicious dish has been handed down from generation to generation.

3 small, fresh chickens, quartered
10 ml (2 tsp) medium-coarse salt
10 ml (2 tsp) red leaf masala
10 ml (2 tsp) peri-peri oil
175 g (³/₄ cup) margarine
6 pieces stick cinnamon
10-12 pineapple slices
1 kg medium potatoes, peeled and
cut into chips
oil for deep-frying

WASH CHICKEN PORTIONS well and drain in a colander. Sprinkle salt and masala on a smooth surface and rub chicken into the mixture.

Transfer to large porcelain or glass bowl and allow to marinate for a few minutes. Add peri-peri oil, turn the chicken a few times and set aside for about 10 minutes.

Heat a heavy-based saucepan or cast-iron roasting pan on medium heat and add margarine. Add the chicken pieces and cinnamon. Allow to brown a little on one side before turning to brown the other side. Small amounts of water can be added as the chicken grills. Do not cover the pan.

Fry pineapple slices in a heavy-based pan on low heat in 15 ml (1 tbsp) chicken oil taken from the roasting pan. Deep-fry potato chips and serve alongside the chicken. A favourite salad and fresh corn on the cob are perfect accompaniments. SERVES 10-12

Labarang Oven-Roast Chicken

We usually serve this meal at Labarang, the Festival of Charity.

1 x 2 kg fresh chicken
10 ml (2 tsp) salt
2,5 ml (¹/₂ tsp) black *or* white pepper
¹/₂ green *or* red pepper, sliced
1 kg medium potatoes, peeled and
sliced or wedged
10 ml (2 tsp) peri-peri oil
10 ml (2 tsp) margarine
125 ml (¹/₂ cup) water
5 ml (1 tsp) ground cinnamon

SEASON CHICKEN WITH a little salt and pepper and allow to stand for about 5 minutes. Rub well with a few pepper slices. Put remaining slices into chicken cavity. Season potatoes with salt and pepper.

Arrange chicken and potatoes in a roasting pan and pour over oil and melted margarine. Add cold water to soften potatoes and cover with foil. Roast in oven at 180 °C for about 40 minutes. Remove foil, reduce temperature to 160 °C and cook until done. Sprinkle with cinnamon 5 minutes before serving. SERVES 8

Labarang Grilled Chickens

First bake the chicken, then grill to crisp the skin.

3 young chickens
1 green pepper, sliced
15 ml (3 tsp) salt
10 ml (2 tsp) red masala
250 g (1 cup) butter *or* margarine
3 pieces stick cinnamon

WASH AND DRAIN chickens. Rub the skin with some of the green pepper and fill the cavities with the remaining slices. Season with salt and red masala and set aside for 30 minutes.

Heat butter or margarine in a heavy-based roasting pan. Add chickens and

cinnamon and bake, covered, for 30 minutes. Remove cover and place under the grill. Baste and grill until tender and golden-brown, adding a little water to the pan if necessary.

Serve with deep-fried sweet potatoes, noodle salad and Malayan Cauliflower (page 55). SERVES 12

Malayan Crumbed Chicken

The chicken is steamed first, then crumbed and fried in oil.

1 kg chicken portions
4 chicken drumsticks
7,5 ml (1¹/₂ tsp) salt
5 ml (1 tsp) ground cinnamon
4 pieces stick cinnamon
375 ml (1¹/₂ cups) dry breadcrumbs
5 ml (1 tsp) cayenne pepper
60 ml (¹/₄ cup) oil
15 ml (1 tbsp) peri-peri oil
1 cardamom pod, split open
3 large eggs, lightly beaten

WASH CHICKEN PIECES, drain and rub with salt and ground cinnamon. Steam in a saucepan in a little water with the stick cinnamon for about 20 minutes. Remove chicken, drain and set aside to cool.

Mix crumbs with cayenne pepper in a bowl. Heat oils and cardamom in a frying pan. Working quickly, dip the chicken first in the egg, then in the crumbs. Fry chicken on low heat until crisp and golden-brown.

Serve with Masala Chips (page 57) and salads. SERVES 6

NOTES

✔ An upside-down colander on top of the pan helps the chicken to crisp.

✔ Another way of coating the chicken with crumbs is to put the breadcrumbs in a plastic or brown paper bag, dropping the chicken into the bag, and shaking it to ensure a good, even coating.

Sweet and Sour Chicken, this page, and Sweet Sultana Yellow Rice, page 54

Devilled Chicken

12 chicken drumsticks
1/2 red *or* green pepper, sliced
7,5 ml (1 1/2 tsp) salt
5 ml (1 tsp) cayenne pepper
7,5 ml (1 1/2 tsp) red leaf masala
75 g (5 tbsp) butter *or* margarine
2 pieces stick cinnamon
250 ml (1 cup) water

WASH DRUMSTICKS WELL. Combine pepper slices, salt, cayenne pepper and masala, sprinkle over chicken, and allow to marinate for about 10 minutes.

Heat a heavy-based roasting pan over medium heat for 5 minutes. Reduce heat to low and add butter. As soon as butter heats up, add drumsticks and cinnamon. Grill in roasting pan, uncovered, for about 15 minutes, then add water. Cover and cook until water has been absorbed. Grill again, uncovered, until done (about 45 minutes). Serve with corn and chips. SERVES 6

Sweet and Sour Chicken

The mixture of tamarind and sugar gives this dish its distinctive sweet-sour flavour.

1 medium-sized chicken, jointed
4 chicken drumsticks
a pinch turmeric
7,5 ml (1 1/2 tsp) tandoori masala
3 cloves garlic, crushed
10 ml (2 tsp) salt
30 ml (2 tbsp) oil
1 large onion, sliced
60 ml (1/4 cup) boiling water
10 ml (2 tsp) sugar
60 g (1/4 cup) tamarind
10 curry leaves
125 ml (1/2 cup) water

WASH AND DRAIN chicken. Mix turmeric, masala, garlic and salt together, rub into chicken, set aside and marinate for about 10 minutes.

Heat oil in shallow, heavy-based pan. Toss in onion and fry until golden-brown. Add chicken and cover the pan for 5 minutes.

Meanwhile, add the boiling water and sugar to the tamarind. Allow to draw, remove lid and stir. Add the tamarind and sugar mixture to the chicken by pouring it through a sieve – scrape sieve with a spoon to let pulp pass through.

Add curry leaves and the cold water to the chicken. Reduce heat, cover and simmer for about 25 minutes until tender, making sure that the onion does not disintegrate.

Serve with Sweet Sultana Yellow Rice (page 54) and Lemon and Kumquat Atjar (page 63). SERVES 6

Sesame Seed Chicken

An interesting flavour combination with the peri-peri oil and the sesame seeds.

1 kg chicken portions
6 drumsticks
15 ml (1 tbsp) salt
10 ml (2 tsp) red masala
10 ml (2 tsp) prepared *or*
home-made chutney
10 ml (2 tsp) tomato sauce
15 ml (1 tbsp) brown vinegar
15 ml (1 tbsp) peri-peri oil
125 g (1/2 cup) soft margarine
60 ml (1/4 cup) sesame seeds

WASH AND DRAIN chicken. Mix the remaining ingredients together, except sesame seeds, and marinate chicken for 2 hours.

Bake in a large roasting pan at 200 °C for about 40 minutes. Add small amounts of water during cooking to prevent burning. Sprinkle over the sesame seeds 15 minutes before the end of the cooking time.

Serve with a favourite noodle salad or salads of your choice. SERVES 6

Poultry Stuffing

30 ml (2 tbsp) white breadcrumbs
500 g sausage meat
(beef sausages without casings)
1 onion, chopped
2,5 ml (1/2 tsp) dried thyme
2,5 ml (1/2 tsp) dried tarragon
2,5 ml (1/2 tsp) fine black pepper
leaf of celery stalk
a pinch ground nutmeg
5 ml (1 tsp) salt
3 dried peaches *or* apple slices,
roughly chopped
1 egg, beaten with 60 ml (4 tbsp) milk

COMBINE ALL THE ingredients to form a fairly stiff mixture. Make sure that the stuffing is tightly packed into the chicken or turkey cavity. STUFFS 1 LARGE CHICKEN OR TURKEY

Sesame Seed Chicken

Grilled Capons

A special dish to delight your family.

3 capons or baby chickens, halved
500 g medium potatoes, peeled
and halved
1/2 green pepper, sliced
10 ml (2 tsp) salt
10 ml (2 tsp) leaf masala
250 g (1 cup) margarine
6 pieces stick cinnamon

WASH AND DRAIN the capons. Marinate capons and potatoes with pepper slices, salt and masala for about 10 minutes. Heat margarine and cinnamon in a heavy-based roasting pan or saucepan, then add capons and potatoes a few at a time.

Grill at 180 °C for about 35 minutes, turning occasionally, until tender. Remove and keep warm until all the capons and potatoes are cooked.

Serve with buttered noodles, corn on the cob and avocado wedges. SERVES 6

Chicken in a Jiffy

*An easy, flavoursome way to
prepare chicken.*

1 x 1 kg chicken braai pack
1/2 green pepper,
seeds removed
10 ml (2 tsp) salt
10 ml (2 tsp) red masala
2,5 ml (1/2 tsp) gharum masala
5 ml (1 tsp) fine black pepper
4 whole cloves
30 ml (2 tbsp) soft margarine
10 ml (2 tsp) flour
2 large Jiffy Cooking Bags

WASH AND DRAIN chicken portions, then rub each portion with the inside of green pepper. Marinate with salt, spices and margarine, and allow to stand for 30 minutes.

Pierce Jiffy bags twice on one side with a fork. Place 5 ml (1 tsp) flour in each bag and shake. Divide marinated chicken into two and place in bags. Secure bags with ties provided and bake at 180 °C on middle shelf of oven for 45 minutes.

Serve with vegetables and deep-fried baby potatoes. SERVES 4

Muscovy Duck Pot Roast

A Muscovy duck has greenish-black plumes with white markings and a red caruncle on the bill. It's a messy duck but tastes so nice!

1 fresh, young Muscovy duck
1/4 red *or* green pepper
10 ml (2 tsp) salt
10 ml (2 tsp) ground black pepper
5 ml (1 tsp) red masala
1 kg small potatoes, peeled
375 ml (1 1/2 cups) oil for
deep-frying
125 g (1/2 cup) margarine
2 sticks cinnamon

THE DUCK MUST be well-plucked and washed under slow-running, cold water. Soak duck in very mildly salted water for 30 minutes. Drain, then marinate by rubbing with red or green pepper first, then salt, black pepper and masala. Set aside.

Meanwhile, deep-fry potatoes in hot oil and set aside. Strain potato oil and store for later use.

Heat margarine in saucepan, add duck with cinnamon sticks on top and grill, uncovered, on medium heat, adding small amounts of water. Reduce heat after 40 minutes and add potatoes to pan.

Serve with a selection of vegetables or salads. SERVES 6

NOTES
✔ To remove burns and stains from pots and pans, cook together 375 ml (1 1/2 cups) boiling water, 5 ml (1 tsp) cream of tartar and a squeeze of lemon juice for 15 minutes, then clean pots with a sponge.
✔ If desired, use the Poultry Stuffing recipe on page 26 to stuff the Labarang Turkey recipe below.

Labarang Turkey

A special dish for Eid or Christmas.

1 x 2 kg turkey
1 small green pepper, sliced
15 ml (1 tbsp) salt
10 ml (2 tsp) leaf masala
375 ml (1 1/2 cups) water
250 g (1 cup) butter *or* margarine,
melted
5 ml (1 tsp) finely ground cinnamon
3 cinnamon sticks
2,5 ml (1/2 tsp) dried thyme
2,5 ml (1/2 tsp) dried tarragon
2,5 ml (1/2 tsp) dried oregano
500 g each sweet potatoes and
potatoes, peeled and thickly wedged
a pinch each fine salt and masala
oil for deep-frying

RUB TURKEY WELL with green pepper, salt and masala. Place in a heavy-based saucepan with water and steam for about 1 hour.

Preheat oven to 180 °C. Transfer turkey to roasting pan and pour melted butter over and inside turkey, then sprinkle with cinnamon. Put cinnamon sticks on the top of the turkey to enhance the flavour. Roast, uncovered, basting occasionally. Mix thyme, tarragon and oregano together and sprinkle over turkey just before serving.

Sprinkle potatoes and sweet potatoes with a pinch of fine salt and masala and deep-fry.

Serve with salads or noodles with canned fruit salad. SERVES 8

Meat Dishes

Meat, usually served with rice, forms the staple diet of the Malay community. The meat, often braised first, is cooked in a variety of ways. Offal is particularly favoured and is considered a delicacy.

Potroast Leg of Lamb

My favourite Eid meal.

1 x 2 kg leg of lamb
10 ml (2 tsp) peri-peri oil
4 cloves garlic, crushed
10 ml (2 tsp) salt
7,5 ml (1½ tsp) pepper
5 ml (1 tsp) red masala
500 ml (2 cups) water
1 small carrot, peeled and sliced
1 kg new potatoes
375 ml (1½ cups) oil

WHEN PURCHASING THE lamb, ask your butcher to remove the gland; alternatively, slit the inside of the leg and remove the gland and cord which is covered by fat. Make a few incisions in the meat before soaking in lukewarm water for 20 minutes. Rub with peri-peri oil, garlic, salt, pepper and masala and place in roasting saucepan with the water. Cook, covered, for 60 minutes on high, then reduce to medium. Add carrot to stock. Baste meat occasionally for 40 minutes or until tender. Add more water during cooking to make a thick gravy. Deep-fry potatoes in hot oil and serve with Spicy Carrots and Gem Squash (page 52). SERVES 6-8

Leftover Farm Special

Don't throw out any not-so-fresh vegetables – use them in this tasty meal.

60 ml (4 tbsp) oil
1 kg stewing beef
2 onions, chopped
500 ml (2 cups) water
salt to taste
10 ml (2 tsp) leaf masala
1 ripe tomato, grated
½ green chilli, chopped
5 carrots, peeled and cut into pieces
250 g green beans, cut into stubs
1 x 225 g tin green peas
1 small spitskop cabbage (curly top), cut into small pieces
500 g potatoes, peeled and wedged

HEAT OIL IN a saucepan and braise meat and onions until medium brown. Add the water, salt, masala, tomato and chilli and simmer until water has cooked away. Now braise a little with small amounts of water.
 Add vegetables, except potatoes, and cook for a further 10 minutes. Add potatoes and cook until done. Serve with Braised Brown Rice (page 54). SERVES 6

OPPOSITE   Potroast Leg of Lamb

Cabbage Meatball Wrap

We call this 'kool frikkadel' – make enough gravy to half cover the parcels.

60 ml (¼ cup) oil
3 marrow bones
1 onion, chopped
2,5 ml (½ tsp) salt
625 ml (2½ cups) water
1 medium spitskop cabbage (curly top)
5 ml (1 tsp) ground black pepper
5 ml (1 tsp) ground nutmeg
4 whole cloves
6 allspice
2 bay leaves
60 g (¼ cup) butter
10 ml (2 tsp) fine, dry breadcrumbs

MEATBALLS
5 slices stale bread, soaked in water
for 5 minutes and squeezed dry
1 kg steak mince
7,5 ml (1½ tsp) salt
1 egg
10 ml (2 tsp) chopped parsley

HEAT OIL IN a large, shallow saucepan and add marrow bones, onion, salt and 250 ml (1 cup) water. Braise until golden-brown.

Separate cabbage into leaves, removing veins but leaving a bit of stalk, and wash well. Add the remaining 375 ml (1½ cups) water to the saucepan. Place cabbage leaves on top of the meat and steam for about 10 minutes, covered, until the leaves are half-cooked and brown. Remove from stove.

To make the meatballs, place bread in a mixing bowl, add mince and remaining meatball ingredients plus 2,5 ml (½ tsp) each of pepper and nutmeg. Mix well using a spoon. The texture must be fairly loose.

Using your hands, shape mince mixture into balls about the size of golf balls. Remove cabbage leaves from the saucepan with a slotted spoon. Place a meatball in the centre of each cabbage leaf, roll up into parcels and set aside on a platter.

Return saucepan to the stove and bring to the boil over medium heat. The moment the gravy begins to cook, return the cabbage parcels to the pan and sprinkle over remaining pepper and nutmeg, cloves, allspice, bay leaves and butter, cut into small pieces. Finally, add the breadcrumbs, cover, and steam on low heat for about 20 minutes.

Serve cabbage parcels on a bed of white rice. SERVES 6

NOTE

✔ To tenderize meat for frying, pour 10 ml (2 tsp) vinegar over the meat, rub it in and leave for 10 minutes. Then pound meat with the bottom of a heavy stoneware mug or saucer (it's an old wive's tale but it works!). Do this a few times, then use as desired.

BELOW   Cabbage Meatball Wrap, this page, served with Long-Grain White Rice, page 54

Curried Meatballs

A fine meal to serve for a Sunday lunch.

SAUCE
60 ml (¹/4 cup) oil
2 onions, chopped
1 piece stick cinnamon
500 ml (2 cups) water
10 ml (2 tsp) tomato sauce
5 ml (1 tsp) masala
7,5 ml (1¹/2 tsp) turmeric
5 ml (1 tsp) ginger paste
5 ml (1 tsp) salt
1 starseed petal (star anise)
15 ml (1 tbsp) brown vinegar
2 bay leaves
5 ml (1 tsp) sugar
3 allspice
10 ml (2 tsp) dried breadcrumbs

MEATBALLS
4 slices stale bread, soaked in water
for 5 minutes and squeezed dry
15 ml (1 tbsp) chopped parsley
nut of butter
1 tomato, cubed
500 g coarse steak mince

TO MAKE THE sauce, heat oil over medium heat and stir-fry three-quarters of the onion. Add cinnamon and water, then add tomato sauce, masala, 5 ml (1 tsp) turmeric, ginger paste, 2,5 ml (¹/2 tsp) salt, starseed petal and vinegar. Mix well and leave to simmer.

Prepare the meatballs by placing bread in a basin and adding 2,5 ml (¹/2 tsp) turmeric, parsley, butter, tomato, remaining 2,5 ml (¹/2 tsp) salt and mince. Mix well but lightly and form into medium-sized balls.

The sauce should be simmering when the meatballs are added to the saucepan. If necessary, add extra water before adding the meatballs. Reduce heat and add bay leaves, sugar, allspice and breadcrumbs. It is important that you do not stir at this stage. Simmer covered, until done (about 15 minutes).

Enjoy with rice and Carrot and Chilli Sambal (page 60). SERVES 4

Braised Steak Mince

I often use this as a roti filling.

60 ml (¹/4 cup) oil
1 large onion, chopped
1 small tomato, blanched, peeled and pulped
1 kg coarse steak mince
1 green pepper, quartered
2,5 ml (¹/2 tsp) red masala
1 small green chilli, chopped
2,5 ml (¹/2 tsp) crushed garlic
10 ml (2 tsp) salt
1 whole clove
4 allspice
500 g small potatoes, peeled and quartered
60 ml (¹/4 cup) water

USING A HEAVY-BASED saucepan, heat oil over a medium heat and toss in the onion. Stir-fry until well browned. Add the remaining ingredients. Stir thoroughly and cook, covered, for 5 minutes, then reduce heat and simmer until potatoes are soft. SERVES 5 AS A MAIN MEAL

Lambs' Hearts and Sours

For those who like offal, this is a dish you'll really enjoy.

4 lambs' hearts, washed and sliced into thin rings
2,5 ml (¹/2 tsp) salt
2,5 ml (¹/2 tsp) leaf masala
250 ml (1 cup) water
60 ml (¹/4 cup) oil
1 medium onion, sliced
4 slices red *or* green pepper
15 ml (1 tbsp) brown vinegar
5 ml (1 tsp) sugar

SPRINKLE SALT AND masala on heart slices. Over a medium heat, cook meat in water for 20 minutes. Now add most of the oil and continue to cook until the meat starts to fry.

Stir continuously and rapidly until light brown, then remove from heat. Cover and set aside in preheated warming drawer.

Using a separate pan, heat the remaining oil and toss in onion. Braise a little, then add sliced pepper, vinegar, sugar and a pinch of salt. Turn off heat. Spoon this mixture over hearts. This is a delicious meal with warm corn on the cob, buttered Brussels sprouts and Light Brown Rolls (page 90). SERVES 3

Malayan Bobotie

60 ml (¹/4 cup) oil
1 medium onion, chopped
4 cloves garlic, slivered
2,5 ml (¹/2 tsp) curry powder
2 bay leaves, torn
5 ml (1 tsp) red masala
10 ml (2 tsp) salt
6 slices stale bread, soaked in water for 5 minutes and squeezed dry
30 ml (2 tbsp) butter *or* margarine
1 kg steak mince
4 eggs

HEAT 15 ML OIL (1 tbsp) in a saucepan over medium heat. Add onion, garlic, curry powder, bay leaves, masala and salt. Reduce heat to low and braise onion lightly. Add bread, stir a couple of times and cook for 5 minutes. Remove from heat and allow to cool.

Stir in butter and mince and transfer to an ovenproof glass dish. Bake at 180 °C for 30 minutes. Beat eggs well, adding 15 ml (1 tbsp) cold water. Remove bobotie from oven and pour egg over the top. Return to oven and bake, uncovered, for 5-10 minutes. Serve with yellow rice and salads. SERVES 8

Special Lasagne

The pasta is homemade, there's no white sauce and the meat is deliciously spiced.

60 ml (¼ cup) oil
1 large onion, chopped
5 cloves garlic, crushed
1 kg coarse steak mince
1 starseed petal (star anise)
½ red or green pepper,
cut into strips
1 x 65 g tin tomato paste
10 ml (2 tsp) medium-coarse salt
7,5 ml (1½ tsp) tandoori masala
2,5 ml (½ tsp) turmeric
10 ml (2 tsp) white sugar
1 small green chilli, chopped
250 ml (1 cup) fresh orange juice
200 g Parmesan *or*
Cheddar cheese, coarsely grated
5 ml (1 tsp) dried oregano
5 ml (1 tsp) dried thyme

PASTA
2 eggs
2 cups flour
2,5 ml (½ tsp) salt
2,5 ml (½ tsp) masala
2,5 ml (½ tsp) dried tarragon
2,5 ml (½ tsp) dried thyme
2,5 ml (½ tsp) dried oregano
375 ml (1½ cups) lukewarm water

FIRST MAKE THE meat sauce. Heat oil in a large saucepan on medium-high. Add onion and garlic and sauté until transparent. Now add mince and cook until well-browned.

Add the rest of the ingredients, except orange juice, cheese, oregano and thyme, and cook for a few minutes, stirring occasionally. Reduce heat to low, add orange juice and simmer for about 10 minutes or until the sauce is fairly thick but not dry. Remove from heat and leave to cool.

To make the pasta, mix all the ingredients together to form a soft, pliable dough. If the dough is too crumbly, add a few drops of water. If it's too wet and sticks to the bowl, add a little extra flour. Roll out on a floured surface as thinly as possible and cut into strips, about 5 cm x 20 cm. Boil water in a deep saucepan. Drop the strips of dough into the boiling water, reduce heat and cook for 5-7 minutes. Remove with a slotted spoon and set aside. Continue in this way until all the dough has been used.

Line a well-greased ovenproof dish with the pasta strips and fill with the meat mixture. Alternatively, layer the meat and pasta, ending with a layer of pasta. Sprinkle over grated cheese, thyme and oregano and heat through on the middle shelf of the oven at 180 °C for about 15 minutes or until cheese has melted.

Serve hot with Beetroot and Onion Salad (page 57) and Cucumber Salad (page 57). SERVES 6

Hazendal Pumpkin

One winter afternoon I saw four Hazendal women returning from the abattoir with offal (which was then given away free) and dividing it amongst themselves – I devised this recipe with them in mind.

2 kg sheep or ox tripe, cleaned
60 ml (¼ cup) oil
2 marrow bones
1 onion, chopped
1 kg pumpkin or hubbard squash,
sliced or cubed
2,5 ml (½ tsp) turmeric
7,5 ml (1½ tsp) salt
1 starseed petal (star anise)
1 chilli or a pinch cayenne pepper
4 slices red *or* green pepper
7,5 ml (1½ tsp) fresh ginger
10 ml (2 tsp) sugar

IT IS IMPORTANT that tripe be well cooked. Sheep tripe takes 2 hours and ox tripe 3 hours to cook in a saucepan, and both will take about 1 hour in a pressure cooker. Cut the tripe into strips about 6 cm x 2 cm and set aside. Heat oil in a broad saucepan over medium heat, add bones and onion and braise until well-browned. Now add the pumpkin, turmeric, salt, starseed and chilli. Cook, uncovered, for about 30 minutes, stirring once or twice. When pumpkin starts drying out, reduce heat and add sliced pepper, ginger, sugar and tripe. Simmer for about 10 minutes – do not add any water unless absolutely necessary. Serve with rice and chutney. SERVES 4-5

Liver and Onion

An all-time favourite Malay supper.

1 kg sheep liver, film removed and cut into thin slices
5 ml (1 tsp) salt
5 ml (1 tsp) ground black pepper
60 ml (¼ cup) vinegar *or*
60 ml (¼ cup) milk
250 ml (1 cup) oil
125 ml (½ cup) cake flour
a pinch ground *or* grated nutmeg
4 small onions, sliced
1 red *or* green chilli, halved

WASH AND DRY the liver. Season with salt and pepper, add vinegar or milk, and set aside for 1 hour.

Heat oil in a skillet over medium heat until medium hot. Remove liver from milk or vinegar and allow excess liquid to drip off. Dip into the flour mixed with nutmeg and fry. Using a fork, turn liver quickly until done. If it is cooked for too long it will become tough.

Braise onions with the chilli in a small pan until golden-brown, then flavour with a little vinegar and sugar. Serve immediately with mashed potatoes and steamed gem squash. SERVES 6

Liver and Onion, page 32

Labarang Corned Beef

My Labarang speciality.

2 kg topside beef
2 litres (8 cups) water
1 bay leaf
1 whole clove
15 ml (1 tbsp) coriander seeds
60 g (¼ cup) saltpetre (obtainable
from a pharmacy)
250 g (1 cup) coarse salt

USING A KNIFE with a sharp point, make about 10 slits in the meat, 2,5 cm deep and wide enough to press spices into them. Boil water and add bay leaf, clove and 5 ml (1 tsp) coriander, slightly crushed.

Wet meat with hands, but do not wash. Working in a broad enamel or porcelain mixing bowl, fill holes in meat first with saltpetre and salt. Be careful that you do not have any open cuts on your hands. Allow meat to stand for 5 minutes, then wet meat again and allow to stand for a further 5 minutes. Lastly insert three-quarters of the coriander seeds and sprinkle remainder on top. Saltpetre melts the moment it makes contact with the wet meat but salt takes a little longer. Leave meat to stand in very cool place overnight and turn every 6 hours.

On the following day, pour in 500 ml (2 cups) cold water. Leave to stand for 2 more days, turning occasionally. On the third day rinse lightly and cook in 1,5 litres (6 cups) water until soft. Dilute water if too salty. If using a pressure cooker, cook for about 1 hour. If using a saucepan, it will take about 2½ hours. Use the same water to boil your vegetables in or steam them. SERVES 6-8

Koue Bokkeveld Special

500 g (2½ cups) dried peas,
soaked overnight
60 ml (¼ cup) oil
1 onion, sliced
1 ox trotter, precooked
½ green pepper, chopped
½ green chilli
1 starseed petal (star anise)
7,5 ml (1½ tsp) salt
10 ml (2 tsp) sugar

RINSE DRIED PEAS well and cook until soft. Remove any shells that rise to the surface, and drain. Heat oil in a saucepan over medium heat. Braise onion until golden-brown. Now add trotter, peas and remaining ingredients to the saucepan and simmer over a very low heat for 10 minutes. Enjoy with chutney and rice. SERVES 6

Curries and Breyanis

A Malay curry is sweeter than an Indian one and is usually served with rice or rotis and sambals. Also very popular, a breyani is a semi-dry dish of rice, spices and meat, chicken or fish, served in one pot.

Akhni

60 ml (¼ cup) oil
1,5 kg mutton thin ribs
2 onions, chopped
6 small pieces stick cinnamon
4 cardamom pods
500 ml (2 cups) water
500 g (2½ cups) parboiled
brown rice
5 ml (1 tsp) turmeric
10 ml (2 tsp) salt
½ green pepper
5 ml (1 tsp) leaf masala
4 whole cloves
10 ml (2 tsp) garlic and ginger paste
1 starseed petal (star anise)
1 red *or* green chilli, halved
5 ml (1 tsp) gharum masala
20 curry leaves and stalks
20 ml (1½ tbsp) tomato sauce
2 thick slices tomato
5 ml (1 tsp) sugar

HEAT OIL IN a large saucepan over medium heat. Arrange meat on the bottom of the saucepan, followed by the onion, 4 pieces stick cinnamon and cardamom pods. Cook without water, uncovered, allowing meat to draw water. Braise until dry. Add the water and continue to cook, covered, on medium heat.

In the mean time, cook rice in rapidly boiling water with turmeric, salt and remaining 2 pieces of stick cinnamon. Drain in colander and steam for 20 minutes. Set aside to cool until later. To save time, the rice can be prepared in advance and kept in the fridge until needed.

Add the remaining ingredients, except rice, to meat mixture, reduce heat to low, and stir gently. When the meat is tender and juicy, mix in the rice. When the meat and rice have heated through, remove from heat.

Serve hot with buttered new potatoes, salads and Tomato and Mint Sambal (page 62). SERVES 8

NOTES

✔ In the Akhni recipe, the curry and rice are served in one pot, which makes it a practical and popular dish when catering for large functions or ceremonies.

✔ To give fish and potatoes a good colour, sprinkle a few drops of lemon juice over them before cooking.

✔ Keep flies out of the kitchen by hanging a tomato plant or a mint sprig from the ceiling. Get rid of ants and cockroaches by sprinkling a mix of salt and borax along the back of shelves.

OPPOSITE   Lamb Cutlet and Brinjal
Curry, page 38

Hout Bay Crayfish Tail Curry

Make sure that the shell and the tail of the crayfish are slit open and the alimentary canal extracted before cooking.

1 x 3 cm block tamarind
125 ml (1/2 cup) boiling water
10 ml (2 tsp) sugar
60 ml (1/4 cup) oil
1 large onion, chopped
45 ml (3 tbsp) tomato purée
5 ml (1 tsp) turmeric
5 ml (1 tsp) red masala
625 ml (2 1/2 cups) water
3 medium, fresh *or* frozen
crayfish tails, quartered
1 small tomato, blanched,
peeled and pulped
5 ml (1 tsp) garlic and ginger paste
1 starseed petal (star anise)
10 curry leaves
5 whole cloves
5 allspice
4 pieces stick cinnamon
4 cardamom pods, split open
5 ml (1 tsp) salt
5 ml (1 tsp) ground jeera (cumin)

SOAK TAMARIND IN the boiling water and sugar for about 2 minutes. Strain and set liquid aside.

Heat oil in broad, heavy-based saucepan over medium heat. Add onion and braise until golden-brown. Add tomato purée, turmeric, masala and 125 ml (1/2 cup) water; reduce heat to low. Add tails, tomato pulp and remaining ingredients, except jeera and tamarind liquid, to saucepan and cook slowly.

Add remaining 500 ml (2 cups) water, jeera and tamarind liquid. Add more sugar to taste, cover and simmer gently. Do not remove lid until ready to serve with fluffy white rice and lemon wedges. SERVES 5

NOTE

✔ Soft fish in a curry will shred easily.

Minced Perlemoen Curry

Vary this dish by adding fried brinjal wedges or early garden peas.

30 ml (2 tbsp) oil
1 medium onion, chopped
1 small tomato, blanched,
peeled and pulped
2 small pieces stick cinnamon
4 allspice
2 whole cloves
2 cardamom pods, split open
2,5 ml (1/2 tsp) garlic and
ginger paste
2,5 ml (1/2 tsp) red masala
a pinch turmeric
a pinch ground jeera (cumin)
5 curry leaves
2,5 ml (1/2 tsp) medium-coarse salt
2 perlemoen, well cleaned and minced

HEAT OIL IN skillet and add onion. Braise until well-browned. Add tomato, then remaining ingredients, including perlemoen. Simmer for 25 minutes over low heat. Perlemoen has natural juices so do not add water unless absolutely necessary. Serve hot on a bed of rice. SERVES 5

Snoek Curry

The dhania (coriander) leaves enhance the flavour of the snoek.

60 ml (1/4 cup) oil
half a small snoek, cut into steaks
10 ml (2 tsp) salt
7,5 ml (1 1/2 tsp) red roasted masala
flour for dusting
4 pieces stick cinnamon
1 large onion, chopped
10 ml (2 tsp) tomato sauce
1 small tomato, blanched, peeled
and pulped
4 slices green pepper
5 ml (1 tsp) crushed garlic
5 ml (1 tsp) turmeric
4 whole cloves
8 allspice
1 starseed petal (star anise)

---

2 cardamom pods, split open
60 g (1/4 cup) tamarind, soaked in
125 ml (1/2 cup) boiling water with
10 ml (2 tsp) sugar
60 g (1/4 cup) green dhania
(coriander) leaves, torn, *or* 10 curry leaves

HEAT 30 ML (2 TBSP) OIL in a heavy-based saucepan over medium heat. Lightly dust fish with salt, 2,5 ml (1/2 tsp) masala and a little flour. Fry lightly, adding more oil if necessary. Remove fish from pan and drain.

Now heat cinnamon and onion in remaining oil. Add tomato sauce and pulp. Reduce heat and add remaining ingredients, except the tamarind and dhania, stirring a few times and adding small amount of water. Allow to simmer. Scoop out some of the sauce and mix with strained tamarind liquid. Arrange fish in saucepan and cover with the sauce and tamarind.

Before serving, add dhania leaves. Serve hot with Braised Brown Rice (page 54). SERVES 6

Tamarind Fish Curry

Red roman or red or white stumpnose can be used instead of Cape salmon.

1 kg Cape salmon, thickly sliced
10 ml (2 tsp) salt
125 ml (1/2 cup) oil
5 cardamom pods, split open
4 pieces stick cinnamon
1 large onion, chopped
5 ml (1 tsp) turmeric
10 ml (2 tsp) leaf masala
500 ml (2 cups) water
20 ml (1 1/2 tbsp) tomato purée
60 g (1/4 cup) tamarind,
soaked in 125 ml (1/4 cup)
boiling water with
10 ml (2 tsp) sugar
20 curry leaves
2 starseed petals (star anise)
4 whole cloves
8 allspice
2 bay leaves

Hout Bay Crayfish Tail Curry, page 36

WASH AND DRY fish. Season with salt. Heat oil over medium heat in a pan and fry fish with 2 cardamom pods until semi-cooked. Remove from heat and allow to cool. Drain oil from fish for further use. Using a broad saucepan and the same oil, add remaining 3 cardamom pods and cinnamon; heat well.

Braise onion, then add turmeric, masala, water and tomato pureé. Bring slowly to the boil and gently add fried fish.

Pour strained tamarind liquid over fish. Add remaining ingredients and stir well, but gently, so as not to break up fish. Allow to simmer over a low heat. Add more water if the sauce is too dry.

A delicious way to serve this dish is with white rice, Braised Tomato (page 52) and Lemon and Brinjal Atjar (page 64). SERVES 6

Chicken Curry
*A meal in itself! Serve with rotis
and a favourite sambal.*

1 kg chicken portions
7,5 ml (1½ tsp) finely chopped
fresh ginger
4 cloves garlic, finely chopped
30 ml (2 tbsp) oil
6 cardamom pods
6 pieces stick cinnamon
1 large onion, finely chopped
30 ml (2 tbsp) tomato purée
5 ml (1 tsp) turmeric
5 ml (1 tsp) leaf masala
250 ml (1 cup) water
10 ml (2 tsp) salt
10 curry leaves
1 starseed petal (star anise)
500 g potatoes, peeled and quartered
375 ml (1½ cups) water
5 ml (1 tsp) barishap
5 ml (1 tsp) ground jeera (cumin)

WASH AND DRAIN chicken well. Marinate with ginger and garlic for a few minutes. Heat oil in a saucepan and add cardamom and cinnamon. Add onion and stir until golden-brown. Now add tomato purée, turmeric, leaf masala and water.

Add chicken, salt, curry leaves and starseed to saucepan with potatoes and cook for 15 minutes.

Add remaining ingredients, reduce heat and stir well but gently to blend ingredients. Allow to simmer for about 30 minutes until the chicken is tender. Add more water if necessary. Serve with rice or Malay Roti (page 92). SERVES 6

NOTES

✔ When using cup measurements, use a standard kitchen cup.

Penang Curry

A fairly dry but flavoursome curry
which originates from the island
of Penang in Java.

1,5 kg lamb cutlet chops, tenderized
with a light mallet
5 ml (1 tsp) turmeric
5 ml (1 tsp) red masala
5 ml (1 tsp) crushed garlic
10 ml (2 tsp) salt
60 ml (¼ cup) oil
2 cardamom pods, crushed
4 small pieces stick cinnamon
1 large onion, sliced lengthwise
250 ml (1 cup) water
15 ml (1 tbsp) brown vinegar
7,5 ml (1½ tsp) sugar
1 starseed petal (star anise)
2 bay leaves
4 whole cloves
6 allspice
10 ml (2 tsp) dry
breadcrumbs

WASH AND DRAIN chops well in colander and allow to stand for 5 minutes. Marinate chops with turmeric, masala and garlic for 1 hour. Add 7,5 ml (1½ tsp) salt. Heat oil in a frying pan and add crushed cardamom. Add chops and fry lightly for 5 minutes on each side. Remove and place in another dish.

In a broad, heavy-based saucepan, add cinnamon and oil from the frying pan and fry onion lightly. Add meat (the onion should partly cover the meat) and cook for 30 minutes in 125 ml (½ cup) water, making sure that the onion is not cooked away. Do not stir. Add rest of water, cover, reduce heat and simmer – this is a semi-dry curry. Pour vinegar into a cup, add sugar and stir well. Pour over the meat with remaining salt, starseed petal and other spices. Stir in breadcrumbs. Enjoy with yellow rice and salads. SERVES 6

Lamb Cutlet and Brinjal Curry

I was honoured to serve this dish to the
Japanese consul, his wife and secretary a
few years ago – it was a great success!

1,5 kg lean lamb cutlets
2 large onions, chopped
30 ml (2 tbsp) chopped green pepper
15 ml (1 tbsp) medium-coarse salt
10 ml (2 tsp) crushed fresh ginger
10 ml (2 tsp) tandoori masala
a pinch turmeric
15 ml (1 tbsp) tomato sauce
125 ml (½ cup) cold water
2 large brinjals, cut into wedges
5 ml (1 tsp) ground jeera (cumin)
1 starseed petal (star anise)
5 ml (1 tsp) sugar
10 curry leaves with stalks

BELOW   Vegetable Curry, page 39,
Samoosas, page 14, and
Apple Sambal, page 60

CUT RIND OF fat off cutlets. Wash well and arrange in a large, shallow, heavy-based saucepan. Top with onion, pepper, salt, ginger, masala, turmeric and tomato sauce. Allow to simmer, covered, over medium heat for about 20 minutes.

Remove lid and stir thoroughly. Add the cold water and brinjal wedges. Reduce heat, cover and simmer for a further 20 minutes. Add remaining spices, sugar and curry leaves. This is a semi-dry dish so there should not be too much sauce but just enough to keep it moist.

Serve with Cinnamon Rice (page 54) and Apple Sambal (page 60). SERVES 8

Black-Eyed Bean Curry

It's well worth making this tasty, nutritious meal, despite the somewhat lengthy procedure.

500 g (2½ cups) black-eyed beans, soaked overnight in boiling water and drained
60 ml (¼ cup) oil
3 pieces stick cinnamon
1 large onion, chopped
500 g shoulder of mutton, cubed
500 g mutton thick rib *or* knuckle
15 ml (1 tbsp) tomato sauce *or* purée
5 ml (1 tsp) turmeric
5 ml (1 tsp) red masala
375 ml (1½ cups) water
10 curry leaves
5 ml (1 tsp) sugar
5 ml (1 tsp) garlic and ginger paste
5 ml (1 tsp) salt
2,5 ml (½ tsp) ground jeera (cumin)
1 starseed petal (star anise)

COOK BEANS IN salted water until soft and set aside. Heat oil in a heavy-based saucepan over medium heat and scorch cinnamon and onion until golden-brown.

Now add meat, tomato sauce or purée, turmeric, masala and 250 ml

(1 cup) water. Cook until liquid has been absorbed. Stir well and add the remaining 125 ml (½ cup) water. Simmer until meat is tender.

Add beans and remaining ingredients, stir thoroughly, reduce heat and simmer covered. SERVES 6

Mung Dhal Curry

Mung Dhal are tiny green peas, also known as Chinese peas.

1 kg tenderized steak, cubed
2 marrow bones
15 ml (1 tbsp) masala
5 ml (1 tsp) turmeric
5 ml (1 tsp) ginger paste
60 ml (¼ cup) oil
1 onion, chopped
3 cardamom pods, split open
4 pieces stick cinnamon
5 ml (1 tsp) salt
½ green pepper
15 ml (1 tbsp) tomato sauce
5 ml (1 tsp) garlic
2 small green chillies, chopped
10 curry leaves
5 ml (1 tsp) sugar
250 ml (1 cup) water
500 g (2½ cups) mung dhal (Chinese peas), soaked overnight in water, drained and cooked until soft
5 ml (1 tsp) ground jeera (cumin)
1 tomato, blanched, peeled and pulped

WASH MEAT AND drain. Mix masala, turmeric and ginger paste together, rub into steak and allow to marinate for a few minutes. Heat oil in a heavy-based saucepan over medium heat. Add onion, cardamom, cinnamon and marrow bones. Braise until golden-brown. Add the remaining ingredients, except the water, mung dhal, jeera and tomato and cook for 30 minutes. Lastly add water, mung dhal, jeera and tomato.

Enjoy this meal with Malay Roti (page 92) or Khitchri Rice (page 54) and a relish of Lemon and Brinjal Atjar (page 64). SERVES 6

Vegetable Curry

A delicious vegetarian curry which can be made with any vegetable in season. As a variation, small hard-boiled eggs can also be added.

½ small spitskop cabbage (curly top), stalks removed and finely shredded
2 baby gem squashes, cut into quarters, pips removed
½ bunch baby carrots, peeled and sliced
3 medium potatoes, peeled and quartered
60 ml (¼ cup) oil
1 piece stick cinnamon
2 cardamom pods, split open
1 small onion, chopped
15 ml (1 tbsp) tomato sauce
1 small tomato, blanched, peeled and pulped
5 ml (1 tsp) leaf masala
5 ml (1 tsp) turmeric
1 starseed petal (star anise)
5 ml (1 tsp) salt
250 ml (1 cup) water
2,5 ml (½ tsp) sugar
2,5 ml (½ tsp) ground jeera (cumin)
8 curry leaves

SOAK VEGETABLES IN cold water until clean, then drain in a colander. Heat oil in a saucepan and braise cinnamon, cardamom and onion until golden-brown. Add tomato sauce, tomato pulp, masala, turmeric, starseed petal and salt. Braise, then add the water.

Add vegetables to the saucepan, stir gently and mix in sugar. Cook, covered, for another 15 minutes on medium heat, then sprinkle jeera over and steam until done, making sure that the dish has a fair amount of gravy. The curry leaves must be added 5 minutes before the dish is ready to serve.

Enjoy with Apple Sambal (page 60) and white rice tinted with a pinch of turmeric and flavoured with one piece of stick cinnamon. SERVES 4

Penslawer

A popular curry even though the tripe takes some time to prepare.

1,5 kg sheep *or* ox tripe, cleaned
1 litre (4 cups) water
60 ml (1/4 cup) oil
2 pieces stick cinnamon
2 cardamom pods, slightly cracked
1 onion, chopped
5 ml (1 tsp) salt
5 ml (1 tsp) turmeric
1 bay leaf, halved
5 ml (1 tsp) red masala
1 starseed petal (star anise)
5 ml (1 tsp) garlic and ginger paste
15 ml (1 tbsp) tomato purée, pulp of
1/2 tomato *or* 10 ml (2 tsp) tomato sauce
8 curry leaves
2,5 ml (1/2 tsp) ground jeera (cumin)

CUT TRIPE INTO 6 cm x 2 cm slices. Cook in water over medium heat. Sheep tripe takes 2 hours and ox tripe 3 hours in a saucepan. Sheep and ox tripe will take about 1 hour to cook in a pressure cooker. Cook the tripe until tender and set aside before using it for the curry.

Heat oil in a heavy-based saucepan. Toss in cinnamon and cardamom. Add onion and scorch until golden-brown. Add salt, tripe and remaining ingredients, except jeera. Simmer for 30 minutes until done.

Finally add jeera and allow to stand for a few minutes before serving with rice and Apple Sambal (page 60). SERVES 5

Chicken Breyani

Since saffron is so expensive, food colouring is used here as a substitute. This adds colour; saffron, however, adds flavour as well as colour.

1 kg chicken portions
6 small drumsticks
2 onions, sliced
15 ml (1 tbsp) oil
250 g (2 1/2 cups) lentils

500 g (2 1/2 cups) uncooked long-grain white rice
10 ml (2 tsp) margarine
4 pieces stick cinnamon
4 cardamom pods, split open
3 green chillies, chopped
12 small eggs, hard-boiled and peeled
10 ml (2 tsp) jeera (cumin) seeds *or* gharum masala
2,5 ml (1/2 tsp) egg yellow food colouring mixed with
125 ml (1/2 cup) boiling water

MARINADE
250 ml (1 cup) buttermilk *or* stirred yoghurt
10 ml (2 tsp) red masala
7,5 ml (1 1/2 tsp) turmeric
15 ml (1 tbsp) peri-peri oil
10 ml (2 tsp) garlic and ginger paste
5 ml (1 tsp) ground cinnamon
15 ml (1 tbsp) salt

WASH CHICKEN. Combine marinade ingredients and marinate chicken for 2 hours. Fry onion in heated oil until golden-brown. Set aside. Cook lentils in rapidly boiling water, drain and set aside. Cook rice, strain, drain, steam and set aside.

Heat margarine in a heavy-based, large saucepan and toss in cinnamon and cardamom. Add chicken and brown on medium heat. Buttermilk and yoghurt burn easily so add small amounts of cold water as it browns. The water will prevent the chicken from sticking to the pan. Cook uncovered for 1 hour and remove from heat.

In a large dish, mix rice, lentils, onion, chillies and chicken. Transfer half of this mixture to the saucepan and heat through. Make holes with a spoon handle in the breyani and insert whole eggs. Sprinkle with half of the jeera. Then add remaining breyani and sprinkle with remaining jeera, egg yellow and water.

Keep covered on low heat until ready to serve with Green Bean Smoor (page 57) and Cinnamon Pumpkin (page 52). SERVES 6

Steak, Kidney and Brinjal Kedgeree

A kedgeree is similar to a breyani in that it's a semi-dry meal with a little gravy.

1 small brinjal, sliced
5 ml (1 tsp) salt
a pinch red leaf masala
60 ml (1/4 cup) oil
500 g (2 1/2 cups) parboiled white rice
3 whole cloves
500 g tenderized steak, cubed
4 lambs' kidneys, soaked in
10 ml (2 tsp) brown vinegar, drained and cubed
1 onion, sliced in rings
1/2 green pepper, sliced into rings
2 cloves garlic, crushed
2 potatoes, peeled and cubed
3 small carrots, peeled and boiled
4 pieces stick cinnamon
6 allspice
1 x 410 g tin whole-kernel corn, drained
2 tomatoes, cut into wedges and sprinkled with a little sugar

PLACE BRINJAL SLICES in lightly salted water to prevent discoloration. Set aside to drain. Sprinkle with 2,5 ml (1/2 tsp) of the salt and the masala. Fry in 30 ml (2 tbsp) oil until tender and set aside.

Boil rice with cloves, strain, steam and set aside to cool.

Heat the remaining 30 ml (2 tbsp) oil in a heavy-based saucepan and add steak and kidney. Cook for 30 minutes, adding water if necessary and stirring occasionally. Add onion, green pepper and garlic, and fry for a further 10 minutes, then add remaining ingredients, except tomato wedges, and remove from heat.

Layer rice, steak and kidney and brinjal in a casserole dish, ending with a layer of meat. If necessary, heat through in the oven before serving with the tomato wedges, Cabbage Smoor (page 56) and Apple Sambal (page 60). SERVES 4-6

Prawn Breyani

*Leaving the shells on the prawns
enhances the flavour of the breyani.*

1 kg fresh or frozen prawns, deveined
7,5 ml (1 ½ tsp) tandoori masala
10 ml (2 tsp) salt
750 g (3 ¾ cups) uncooked
long-grain white rice
1 small onion, chopped
375 ml (1 ½ cups) oil
4 green *or* red pepper slices
2 pieces stick cinnamon
1 starseed petal (star anise)
4 cardamom pods, split open
1 large onion, sliced
5 ml (1 tsp) turmeric
15 ml (1 tbsp) tomato sauce
5 ml (1 tsp) garlic and ginger paste
200 ml (¾ cup) cold water
5 whole cloves
5 ml (1 tsp) gharum masala

WASH PRAWNS AND marinate with masala and salt. Set aside.

Cook rice in rapidly boiling salted water in a broad saucepan. Drain and set aside. Toss the small chopped onion into 10 ml (2 tsp) warm oil and fry lightly until golden-brown. Add pepper slices, a small piece of stick cinnamon and starseed petal. Remove from the pan when just done.

Using a heavy-based pan over medium heat, lightly fry the prawns in the remaining oil with 1 crushed cardamom pod until all the prawns have been fried. Set aside.

Using only 30 ml (2 tbsp) of the oil that the prawns were fried in, braise large chopped onion until golden-brown. Add remaining ingredients, except cloves and gharum masala. Stir a few times and turn off heat.

Dish out three-quarters of the sauce into the pot, then layer rice, prawns and another layer of rice in the pot, sprinkling cloves and gharum masala over. Slow-steam for 12-15 minutes, then remove from heat and serve with a favourite sambal and Braised Tomato (page 52). SERVES 6

Prawn Breyani

Bredies and Stews

A bredie is a type of stew, slowly simmered – the type of vegetable used gives it its name. Stews are favoured as every-day meals, with a variety of ingredients used and always deliciously spiced.

Tomato Bredie

A very popular dish with Cape Malays, it is best made with fresh, ripe tomatoes. Tomato paste must be added for flavour if canned tomatoes are used. Use 1 x 410 g tin tomatoes and 5 ml (1 tsp) tomato paste instead of fresh tomatoes.

1 kg stewing beef, cubed
60 ml (¼ cup) oil
1 onion, chopped
3 marrow bones
500 g tomatoes, blanched, peeled and pulped
10 ml (2 tsp) tomato paste
5 ml (1 tsp) salt
15 ml (1 tbsp) sugar
1 green chilli, chopped
¼ green pepper, sliced
1 kg small or medium potatoes, peeled and halved
2,5 ml (½ tsp) turmeric
2,5 ml (½ tsp) leaf masala

WASH AND DRAIN meat. Heat oil in a large saucepan on medium heat and toss in beef, onion and bones and braise until well browned.

Now add tomato, tomato paste, salt, sugar, chilli, pepper slices and potatoes. Stir well. Cook for 20 minutes, then reduce heat. Add turmeric and masala; continue to simmer, uncovered, until meat is tender.

Serve with Long-Grain White Rice (page 54). SERVES 6

Tomato-Chicken Bredie

15 ml (1 tbsp) oil
1 medium onion, chopped
1 kg chicken drumsticks
250 g chicken necks, well-washed
500 g ripe tomatoes, blanched, peeled and roughly chopped
½ green chilli, chopped
5 ml (1 tsp) salt
5 ml (1 tsp) tomato paste
a pinch turmeric
10 ml (2 tsp) sugar
1 starseed petal (star anise)
5 ml (1 tsp) dried thyme

HEAT OIL IN a saucepan over medium heat. Toss in onion and braise until golden-brown. Add chicken portions and braise for 10 minutes. Add remaining ingredients, except thyme, and simmer, uncovered, for about 45 minutes.

Lastly add thyme, remove from stove and serve hot with Lemon and Kumquat Atjar (page 63) and Cinnamon Rice (page 54). SERVES 6

OPPOSITE   Waterblommetjie and Celery Bredie, page 47, and Cinnamon Rice, page 54

Baby Green Pea Bredie

This one has an added kick from the chilli.

500 g mutton knuckles
1 medium onion, chopped
10 ml (2 tsp) medium-coarse salt
about 500 ml (2 cups) water
15 ml (1 tbsp) oil
500 g lamb cutlets
1 small starseed petal (star anise)
5 ml (1 tsp) red masala
5 ml (1 tsp) sugar
500 g fresh baby peas, shelled, *or*
frozen peas
1 green chilli, chopped
500 g new potatoes
5 ml (1 tsp) dried thyme

SET A HEAVY-BASED saucepan on medium heat. Add knuckles, onion, salt and 250 ml (1 cup) water and cook until dry. Then add oil and braise until lightly browned. Add cutlets and braise further with a little more water until food has browned completely.

Add remaining ingredients, except thyme and remaining water, and simmer, uncovered, for 45 minutes or until tender. Add thyme and the remaining 250 ml (1 cup) water 15 minutes before the end of cooking time. Reduce heat and simmer.

Serve hot with Long-Grain White Rice (page 54) and Apple Sambal (page 60). SERVES 6

N O T E

✔ The heavier the pot, the lower the heat of the oven plate should be.

Lazy Housewife's Green Bean Bredie

A lazy housewife doesn't like stringing beans – if possible, buy the Lazy Housewife variety of beans.

1 kg lamb shoulder
500 g thin lamb rib
60 ml (¼ cup) oil
1 medium onion, sliced
500 ml (2 cups) water
1 kg fresh green beans, cut
whichever way you prefer
500 g medium potatoes, peeled and
cut into wedges
7,5 ml (1½ tsp) salt
2,5 ml (½ tsp) sugar
1 red *or* green chilli, quartered
a pinch ground jeera (cumin)

CUT MEAT INTO suitably-sized pieces. Heat oil and brown meat until golden-brown before adding onion and 250 ml (1 cup) water.

Simmer until tender, then add beans and potatoes, salt, sugar and chilli. Stir thoroughly and add the remaining water. Finally add jeera and cover the saucepan. Simmer on low heat for 20 minutes.

Serve with rice and Beetroot and Onion Salad (page 57). SERVES 6

> ### NOTES
>
> ✔ Fast-cook meat only if water has been added to the meat in the pot.
> ✔ To prevent the windy after effects of eating cabbage, soak in boiling water for 30 minutes before adding it to the saucepan.
> ✔ Roll a lemon between your hands for a few seconds before cutting or squeezing it – it will give you more juice.
> ✔ When purchasing trotters and tripe, make sure they are clean. Trotters must be split open between the hooves and the gland removed. Soak for 1 hour before cooking.

Lamb Tail and Cabbage Bredie

A good meal to add to the winter diet sheet!

1 spitskop cabbage (curly top)
3 potatoes, peeled and quartered
60 ml (¼ cup) oil
1 onion, chopped
6 lamb cutlets
4 lambs' tails
125 ml (½ cup) water
5 ml (1 tsp) salt
a pinch turmeric
1 green chilli, chopped
2,5 ml (½ tsp) sugar

START BY SEPARATING the cabbage leaves, cutting away the stalks in the centre. Take two leaves at a time, roll and cut into thin ribbon-like shreds and immerse in a basin of cold water. Now add the potatoes to the cabbage and leave to stand.

Heat oil in a large saucepan, add onion and braise until golden-brown. Add cutlets and tails and braise over medium heat until well browned. Then add half the water.

Meanwhile, rinse cabbage and potatoes well, divide into two portions so that any sand can be washed out thoroughly, then drain. Place cabbage, potatoes, meat and remaining ingredients, except water, in saucepan Stir thoroughly. Steam for 10 minutes, pour over remaining water and simmer for a further 20 minutes.

Enjoy with Apple Sambal (page 60) or Apricot and Peach Chutney (page 63) and Long-Grain White Rice (page 54). SERVES 6

BELOW   Lazy Housewife's Green Bean Bredie, page 44, and Beetroot and Onion Salad, page 57

Baby Carrot and Turnip Bredie, page 47

Cabbage and Sweet Turnip Bredie

Prepare this bredie for special occasions.

1 medium spitskop cabbage
(curly top)
60 ml (¼ cup) oil
500 g mutton knuckles
500 g thick lamb rib
1 onion, chopped
1 bunch sweet turnips (kohlrabi),
peeled and cut into thin, short stalks
250 ml (1 cup) water
5 ml (1 tsp) salt
2,5 ml (½ tsp) cayenne pepper
1 medium potato, peeled and quartered
5 ml (1 tsp) sugar
a pinch turmeric

WITH A SHARP knife, remove leaves from cabbage head. In a V pattern, cut away the thick centre stalks of the leaves. Stack in a colander. Wash under slow-running water to remove all sand and dirt. Cut cabbage into thin strips, toss into cold water and leave to stand.

Heat oil in a large saucepan over medium heat. Add meat and onion and cook, covered. Add a little cold water if the meat starts to stick. Allow the meat to braise for about 10 minutes, then add turnips, water, salt and cayenne pepper. Cook for 5 minutes before adding potatoes, cabbage, sugar and turmeric. Cook uncovered for a few minutes and give a good stir, making sure that the potatoes are covered by the turnips and cabbage. When the cabbage has dried out, cover saucepan and reduce heat. Simmer until done.

Serve with Long-Grain White Rice (page 54) and Cucumber Salad (page 57). SERVES 6

NOTE

✔ A pinch of turmeric added to a tomato stew or bredie gives it a lovely rich colour.

Waterblommetjie and Celery Bredie

We call waterblommetjies 'watereendjies' as the plants look like little ducks floating on the water.

1 kg fresh waterblommetjies
60 ml (¼ cup) oil
1,5 kg leg of lamb, cubed
1 large onion, chopped
7,5 ml (1½ tsp) salt
1 green or dried chilli *or*
a pinch cayenne pepper
1 starseed petal (star anise)
2,5 ml (½ tsp) red masala
2 celery leaves with stalks,
roughly chopped
10 ml (2 tsp) dry breadcrumbs

REMOVE TINY FLOWERS from centre of waterblommetjies, rinse them in hot water and set aside. Heat oil slightly, add meat cubes and onion and braise until golden-brown.

Now add salt, chilli or cayenne pepper, starseed and masala. Reduce heat and add waterblommetjies, celery and breadcrumbs and cook for a further 30 minutes or until the meat is tender and succulent.

Remove from heat and serve piping hot with rice and Apple and Dhania Sambal (page 62). SERVES 6

Baby Carrot and Turnip Bredie

3 baby carrots, peeled
and cut into strips
1 bunch baby turnips,
peeled and cut into strips
500 g thin lamb rib
500 g shoulder of mutton, cubed
1 mutton leg chop, cubed
1 onion, chopped
30 ml (2 tbsp) oil
½ chilli, chopped
1 starseed petal (star anise)
5 ml (1 tsp) salt
500 ml (2 cups) water
5 ml (1 tsp) sugar

IMMERSE CARROTS AND turnips in cold water, drain and set aside. Wash and drain meat.

Heat a heavy-based saucepan over medium heat and add meat and onion. Add oil and braise until well browned, then add carrots and cook for 5 minutes.

Add turnips and remaining ingredients, except sugar. Stir and simmer for about 20 minutes. More water can be added if necessary. Lastly add sugar, stir thoroughly and remove from heat.

Serve with Long-Grain White Rice (page 54) and Carrot and Quince Sambal (page 62). SERVES 6

Cabbage and Celery Bredie

Turnips can also be added here if you like.

2 marrow bones
1 large onion, chopped
625 ml (2½ cups) water
1 kg brisket, cut into portions
500 g topside, cut into portions
4 medium potatoes, peeled and
quartered
1 large spitskop cabbage (curly top)
¼ bunch celery leaves, torn
1 green chilli, halved
1 starseed petal (star anise)
5 ml (1 tsp) sugar
7,5 ml (1 ½ tsp) medium-coarse salt
a pinch turmeric

PLACE THE MARROW bones in a saucepan together with onion and 250 ml (1 cup) water and cook, uncovered, for about 15 minutes. Add well-washed meat with a further 250 ml (1 cup) water. Cover saucepan and cook until almost dry. Uncover and allow meat to braise a little until well browned. Add small amounts of water to the meat to prevent burning during this process.

Add potatoes with 125 ml (½ cup) water and simmer for 5 minutes before adding cabbage and the remaining ingredients. Stir thoroughly and cover saucepan for 5 minutes before uncovering again and cooking until done.

Serve with Long-Grain White Rice (page 54). SERVES 8

Brown Lentil Stew

Serve with Long-Grain White Rice (page 54) and Lemon and Brinjal Atjar (page 64).

500 g (2½ cups) brown lentils
60 ml (¼ cup) oil
2 marrow bones
1 kg stewing beef
1 onion, chopped
½ green pepper, chopped
2,5 ml (½ tsp) crushed chillies *or*
1 dry red chilli
5 ml (1 tsp) salt
1 tomato, blanched, peeled
and pulped
5 ml (1 tsp) sugar
2 whole cloves
6 allspice
250 ml (1 cup) water

EMPTY LENTILS ONTO a smooth surface and remove grit and dust. Place lentils in a sieve and rinse thoroughly. Now place lentils in a saucepan with enough boiling water to cover them. Boil for about 45 minutes, strain through sieve and set aside.

Heat oil in a heavy-based saucepan, add meat and top with onion. Braise until browned, about 40 minutes, then add chopped pepper, chilli and salt. Add tomato and remaining ingredients plus lentils. Simmer, covered, over low heat for about 20 minutes. SERVES 6

Brown Stew
A winter's day special!

500 g mutton knuckles, cut into
suitably-sized pieces
2 marrow bones
500 g mutton ribs
1 kg shoulder of mutton
2,5 ml (½ tsp) red masala
875 ml (3½ cups) water
1 large onion, chopped
6 strips green pepper, chopped
1 slice tomato
7,5 ml (1½ tsp) medium-coarse salt
5 ml (1 tsp) ground black pepper
1 green chilli, chopped
10 ml (2 tsp) fine, dry breadcrumbs
15 ml (1 tbsp) oil
1 kg new potatoes, unpeeled

WASH MEAT WELL, drain, season
with masala and set aside. In a shallow, heavy-based saucepan, place
meat, 625 ml (2½ cups) water and
remaining ingredients, except potatoes. Cover saucepan and cook on
medium heat until water has evaporated. The meat should be braised
until well-browned.

Add whole potatoes and the remaining 250 ml (1 cup) water, enough to
cover the stew. Reduce heat and
simmer until done and the sauce is
fairly thick.

Serve with Long-Grain Brown Rice
(page 54) and Apple Sambal (page
60). Sweetcorn Puffs (page 94) and
a cup of filter coffee round off the
meal. SERVES 8

> **NOTE**
>
> ✔ Instead of soaking sugar beans
> overnight to swell them, pour boiling water
> over them and leave to stand in the sun
> for a couple of hours.

Cape Farm Dumpling Stew
A favourite brown stew from my child-
hood – also known as 'Poor Man's Stew'.

60 ml (¼ cup) oil
1 kg stewing beef *or* tenderized
steak, cubed
1 onion, chopped
750 ml (3 cups) water
5 ml (1 tsp) salt
¼ green pepper, sliced
6 allspice
2 whole cloves
2,5 ml (½ tsp) sugar
5 ml (1 tsp) pepper
4 carrots, peeled, quartered
and precooked

DUMPLINGS
250 ml (1 cup) self-raising flour
5 ml (1 tsp) butter *or* margarine
a pinch ground nutmeg

HEAT OIL AND braise meat and onion
until golden-brown. Add 250 ml
(1 cup) water (less if using tenderized steak) to avoid burning. When
meat has browned, add a further
500 ml (2 cups) water; reduce heat to
low. Allow to bubble, then add salt.

To make the dumplings, make a
paste with the flour, butter and
nutmeg and some of the meat stock,
cooled, and stir quickly. Drop
spoonfuls of paste into the stew, add
the remaining ingredients, except
the carrots, and simmer until the
dumplings are done.

Now add carrots to enhance the
flavour and cook until done. Do not
allow to cook dry.

Serve immediately with rice and
Quince Sambal (page 62). SERVES 6

Dried Pea Stew
Another very old recipe, perfect for
a wet winter's day.

500 g (2 ½ cups) dried peas, soaked
and drained
500 ml (2 cups) boiling water
60 ml (¼ cup) oil
1 kg stewing beef
1 shin bone *or* 2 marrow bones
1 onion, chopped
625 ml (2½ cups) cold water
1 dry red chilli
5 ml (1 tsp) cayenne pepper *or*
crushed chillies
5 ml (1 tsp) salt
1 starseed petal (star anise)
2,5 ml (½ tsp) red masala
10 ml (2 tsp) sugar

BOIL THE PEAS in the boiling water,
drain and set aside. Heat oil in a
heavy-based saucepan over medium
heat, add the meat and onion and
cook for a few minutes.

Now add 375 ml (1½ cups) cold
water and cook until the water has
cooked away and the meat has braised
to a golden-brown.

Add a little water to the sizzling
saucepan to loosen the meat. Stir
well. Allow to braise two to three
times until well browned. Add a further 250 ml (1 cup) water and cook,
adding the peas and the remaining
ingredients. Reduce heat to low and
simmer for 10 minutes.

Serve with Long-Grain White Rice
(page 54) topped with home-made
chutney. SERVES 6

> **NOTES**
>
> ✔ As an alternative, use ox trotter sectioned
> by the butcher, well washed and cooked with
> onions into a smoor. Combine with remaining
> ingredients and serve with chutney.
> ✔ Food such as marrow, pumpkin, drum-
> head cabbages and watery tomatoes
> should be cooked, uncovered, until dry
> enough. Cover when making bredies.

Cape Farm Dumpling Stew, page 48, Quince Sambal, page 62, and Long-Grain White Rice, page 54

Oxtail and Sugar Bean Stew

The oxtail needs to be cooked a long time to ensure that it's tender.

500 g (2½ cups) sugar beans
500 g brisket, cubed
1 small oxtail, sectioned
1 medium onion, chopped
560 ml (2¼ cups) water
30 ml (2 tbsp) oil
¼ red *or* green pepper, sliced
1 small tomato, blanched, peeled and pulped
7,5 ml (1½ tsp) salt
2,5 ml (½ tsp) dried thyme
1 clove garlic, crushed
1 starseed petal (star anise)

TO SWELL THE BEANS, soak and leave for 3 hours or overnight in boiling water. First cook in boiling water for 30 minutes, then drain. Add a pinch bicarbonate of soda while cooking beans to soften them, then cook in more water until tender and drain again. Some of the stock can be retained for the meat. Be careful not to boil too long as it will turn into soup instead of stew.

Heat a heavy-based saucepan over medium heat. Spread brisket and oxtail on the base of the saucepan. Top with onion and 500 ml (2 cups) water and cook until all the water has cooked away. Add oil, braise, then 60 ml (¼ cup) water until meat and tail are tender. More water can be added if meat is still tough and needs further cooking.

Add beans and remaining ingredients. Stir through and simmer slowly for 10 minutes. Serve with white rice and Apricot and Peach Chutney (page 63). SERVES 6

N O T E

✔ A mixture of cold water and vinegar will rid pots of any cooking odours. Leave the mixture in the pot overnight.

Lamb Trotter and Tomato Stew

To prepare the trotters, carefully slit the hoof and remove the tiny gland if it has not already been done. Or ask your butcher to do it for you. Soak for 30 minutes in lukewarm, salted water.

12 lamb trotters, prepared (see above)
60 ml (¼ cup) oil
1 onion, chopped
500 g tomatoes, blanched and peeled
10 ml (2 tsp) salt
10 ml (2 tsp) tomato paste
30 ml (2 tbsp) sugar
1 starseed petal (star anise)
½ green chilli, halved
¼ green pepper, chopped

COOK THE PREPARED trotters in water for 2 hours in a saucepan or 1 hour in a pressure cooker.

Heat oil over medium heat and add onion. Braise until golden-brown, then add trotters, tomatoes and salt and cook for 10 minutes. When adding trotters, do not add the stock it was boiled in unless necessary. Reduce heat and add remaining ingredients. Cook, uncovered, for 10-20 minutes.

Delicious served with Long-Grain White Rice (page 54) and Apple Sambal (page 60). SERVES 6

Cape Carrot Stew

This stew is traditionally served at funerals.

60 ml (¼ cup) oil
1 onion, chopped
500 g shoulder of mutton, washed and drained
500 g mutton knuckles, washed and drained
2 marrow bones, washed and drained
2 bunches young carrots, peeled and sliced
3 medium potatoes, peeled and quartered
5 ml (1 tsp) salt

4 whole cloves
4 allspice
½ red *or* green chilli, chopped
5 ml (1 tsp) sugar
a pinch grated nutmeg
2,5 ml (½ tsp) white *or* black pepper
60 ml (¼ cup) chopped parsley

HEAT OIL IN a saucepan over medium heat. Add onion and meat and cover. Allow meat to braise, then add small quantities of water until meat is sufficiently browned.

Now add carrots, potatoes, salt, cloves, allspice, chilli and 250 ml (1 cup) water. Simmer for 10 minutes, stirring occasionally, and reduce heat. Now add sugar, nutmeg, pepper and parsley and simmer until done.

Frozen or fresh peas can be added to this dish if desired. If less gravy is preferred, make the carrot stew into a bredie by cooking until semi-dry. SERVES 5

Grandma's Sago Stew

I grew up with my grandma and spent much of my childhood helping her in the kitchen – this is one of her special winter stews.

500 g chump chops
500 g mutton flat ribs
60 ml (¼ cup) oil
1 onion, chopped
about 375 ml (1½ cups) water
7,5 ml (1½ tsp) salt
3 medium potatoes, peeled and sliced
185 ml (¾ cup) sago, soaked in water for 2 hours
½ red *or* green pepper, chopped
5 allspice
3 whole cloves
½ red *or* green chilli, torn
5 ml (1 tsp) black *or* white pepper
a pinch grated nutmeg
1 starseed petal (star anise)
juice of ½ lemon
2 sprigs celery, torn
60 ml (¼ cup) chopped parsley

Lamb and Pumpkin Stew

CUT MEAT INTO suitably-sized pieces. Wash thoroughly and drain. Heat oil over medium heat until very warm. First add meat, then onion and braise until golden-brown and dry. Add a little water to brown onion, then add 250 ml (1 cup) water, salt and potatoes. Spread meat and potatoes evenly in the pot and cook for 10 minutes.

Reduce heat to low. Top meat and potatoes with sago and add 125 ml (½ cup) water. It is important that you do not stir at this stage – the sago must not be disturbed on top or else it will stick to the pot. Cover and steam for 15 minutes. Add remaining spices, lemon juice, celery and lastly the parsley. Stir the mixture lightly once or twice while simmering for 20 minutes.

Enjoy this meal with home-made chutney. SERVES 6

Lamb and Pumpkin Stew

The secret ingredient in this tasty stew is the ginger which enhances the flavour of the pumpkin. Make sure the pumpkin has a rich, orange skin.

60 ml (¼ cup) oil
3 marrow bones
375 ml (1½ cups) cold water
500 g shoulder of mutton
500 g mutton knuckles
1 onion, chopped
1 red *or* green chilli, torn
10 ml (2 tsp) salt
10 ml (2 tsp) brown *or* white sugar
1 kg pumpkin, peeled, washed and cubed
1 walnut-sized piece of fresh ginger, crushed
a pinch turmeric
½ red or green pepper, sliced
1 starseed petal (star anise)

COOK THIS DISH uncovered. Heat oil in a heavy-based saucepan on medium heat, add marrow bones and 250 ml (1 cup) water and cook for 15 minutes.

Add the rest of the meat that has been cut to the desired size. Top it with onion. Add a further 125 ml (½ cup) water. Simmer until dry, making sure that it does not burn.

Now add 60 ml (¼ cup) water two to three times until the meat is medium brown. Add chilli, salt, sugar and pumpkin. Stir thoroughly. If the pumpkin draws its own water, do not add extra water.

Cook for 15 minutes, then toss in ginger, turmeric and sliced pepper. Stir and simmer on low heat unless it needs drying out.

Enjoy this meal with Long-Grain White Rice (page 54) and home-made chutney. SERVES 6

Rice, Vegetables and Salads

One of the most important dishes on the Malay table, rice can be served with almost any meal! Vegetables are often smoored (braised in oil or fat); salads are preferred accompaniments to curries and grills.

Braised Tomato

A warm dish that goes well with fish.

30 ml (2 tbsp) oil
1 medium onion, sliced
4 tomatoes, blanched, peeled and chopped
3 slices green pepper
sugar to taste
2,5 ml (½ tsp) leaf masala

HEAT OIL IN a pan and braise onion. Add tomatoes, green pepper with sugar to taste and masala, and stir-fry for about 10 minutes until tomato is tender. Serve with a fish, chicken or meat dish of your choice. SERVES 4

N O T E

✔ Blanch tomatoes by plunging into boiling water to loosen the skins.

Spicy Carrots and Gem Squash

The spicy tang of nutmeg enhances the understated flavours of the carrots and squash. Gem squash halves can also be cooked until tender and filled with early garden peas and corn kernels.

½ bunch baby carrots, peeled and sliced
3 young gem squashes, halved and pips removed
2,5 ml (½ tsp) salt
nut of butter *or* margarine
a pinch ground *or* grated nutmeg

IN A LARGE saucepan, steam the carrots and squash together in a little boiling water with salt and butter or margarine. When softened, serve sprinkled with nutmeg. SERVES 6

Cinnamon Pumpkin

The perfect vegetable to serve alongside a mutton stew.

125 ml (½ cup) cold water
500 g pumpkin, peeled and thickly wedged
30 ml (2 tbsp) soft butter
2 cinnamon sticks *or* 5 ml (1 tsp) ground cinnamon
5 ml (1 tsp) soft brown sugar
5 ml (1 tsp) white sugar

PLACE WATER IN a heavy-based saucepan and spread pumpkin over the base in about two layers. Top with remaining ingredients and slow-steam on low heat until soft. SERVES 6

OPPOSITE   Spicy Carrots and Gem Squash, Cinnamon Pumpkin and Braised Tomato

Savoury Rice

A meal in itself or serve as a side dish – brown rice flavoured with chillies give it added zest.

500 g (2½ cups) uncooked long-grain brown rice
15 ml (1 tbsp) salt
30 ml (2 tbsp) oil
2 pieces stick cinnamon
1 large onion, sliced
30 ml (2 tbsp) soft butter
½ red or green pepper, shredded
125 ml (½ cup) celery leaves, torn
1 x 410 g tin whole-kernel corn, drained
2 small green chillies, torn
2,5 ml (½ tsp) red masala
2,5 ml (½ tsp) dried thyme
125 g screw noodles (optional)
5 ml (1 tsp) oil (if using noodles)

BOIL RICE IN water with 10 ml (2 tsp) salt. Strain and steam in a colander over rapidly boiling water.

Heat the oil and cinnamon in a saucepan. Toss in onion and stir-fry until golden-brown; set aside.

Heat butter and stir-fry shredded pepper and celery leaves for a few minutes. Add rice, onion mixture, corn and chillies. Transfer to a heavy-based saucepan. Add masala and thyme. Remove from heat and place in a warming drawer.

If using noodles, cook in rapidly boiling water with remaining salt and the oil for 15 minutes. When *al dente*, drain and add to rice. SERVES 4-6

Cinnamon Rice

Cinnamon rice is a delicious accompaniment to any fish, meat or chicken dish.

1,5 litres (6 cups) water
a pinch turmeric
500 g (2½ cups) uncooked long-grain white rice
2 pieces stick cinnamon
15 ml (1 tbsp) salt

IN A DEEP saucepan, boil water and add turmeric, then remaining ingredients, and allow to cook rapidly for 10 minutes. Turn down heat and cook slowly until rice is tender. Strain and steam in a colander over rapidly boiling water for 10 minutes. SERVES 4-6

Khitchri Rice

To save on cooking time, soak the red lentils in water for about an hour beforehand.

500 g (2½ cups) uncooked long-grain white rice
1 litre (4 cups) boiling water
10 ml (2 tsp) salt
60 g (¼ cup) red lentils
4 pieces stick cinnamon

BOIL RICE IN salted, boiling water with the lentils and cinnamon for about 20 minutes or until done. Drain, rinse and steam on medium heat for 10-15 minutes. Serve hot. SERVES 4-6

Long-Grain White or Brown Rice

No curry or bredie would be complete without rice.

500 g (2½ cups) uncooked long-grain white *or* brown rice
15 ml (1 tbsp) medium-coarse salt
1 litre (4 cups) boiling water

STEAM WHITE RICE for 20 minutes and brown rice for 25-30 minutes over boiling salted water. The bottom of the colander should not touch the water.

This basic recipe can be livened up by adding a piece of stick cinnamon during steaming. SERVES 6

Sweet Sultana Yellow Rice

Instead of using cinnamon, add a few drops of vanilla essence with 2,5 ml (½ tsp) ground cardamom.

500 g (2½ cups) parboiled long-grain white rice
1 litre (4 cups) boiling water
2,5 ml (½ tsp) turmeric
4 small pieces stick cinnamon
10 ml (2 tsp) salt
30 ml (2 tbsp) butter
60 ml (¼ cup) sultanas
15 ml (1 tbsp) sugar

ADD RICE TO boiling water, then add turmeric, cinnamon and salt. Boil for 20 minutes, adding more water if necessary. When rice is tender, strain under cold running water. Steam rice in colander over 2 litres (8 cups) rapidly boiling water for 10 minutes. Return rice to pan on low heat and add butter.

Finally add sultanas and sugar, stir well, steam until sultanas are a little plump, and serve hot. SERVE 4-6

Braised Brown Rice

A wholesome alternative to white rice.

500 g (2½ cups) uncooked brown rice
1 litre (4 cups) boiling water
10 ml (2 tsp) salt
10 ml (2 tsp) oil
1 small onion, sliced
1 piece stick cinnamon

COOK RICE IN rapidly boiling, salted water for 10 minutes, then simmer for a further 10 minutes. Strain and steam in a colander over boiling water.

Heat oil in a saucepan and add onion and stick cinnamon. Fry onion until golden-brown. Add steamed rice to onion mixture, mix well and allow to heat through for about 5 minutes. Serve hot. SERVES 6

Khitchri Rice (left) and Savoury Rice (right), page 54

Malayan Cauliflower

Traditional cauliflower cheese seasoned with masala makes this a hot favourite.

1 medium cauliflower
2,5 ml (¹/₂ tsp) medium-coarse salt
10 ml (2 tsp) cornflour
375 ml (1¹/₂ cups) milk
60 g (¹/₄ cup) butter
30 ml (2 tbsp) fresh double cream
60 g (¹/₄ cup) finely grated Parmesan
or Cheddar cheese
a pinch leaf masala

WASH CAULIFLOWER UNDER slow-running cold water. Steam whole cauliflower in a little water over low heat with 2,5 ml (¹/₂ tsp) salt for about 20 minutes or until just tender. Carefully lift cauliflower from the saucepan with slotted spoons and place on an ovenproof platter.

Blend cornflour and milk into paste with a pinch of salt. Heat butter in shallow saucepan. Add cornflour paste and stir until smooth, then stir in cream, blending well. Remove from heat and allow to cool.

Pour sauce over cauliflower, top with cheese and masala, and bake on middle shelf of oven at 200 °C until golden-brown. SERVES 4

NOTES

✔ A few drops of lemon juice added to cauliflower or potatoes while boiling will whiten them.
✔ It is healthier to steam vegetables rather than to boil them.

Glazed Carrots

These are always popular served with stews or bredies.

1 kg baby carrots, scraped
and washed
250 ml (1 cup) water
5 ml (1 tsp) golden syrup
2,5 ml (¹/₂ tsp) salt
1 piece stick cinnamon
5 ml (1 tsp) soft brown sugar
5 ml (1 tsp) white sugar

PLACE CARROTS IN a shallow saucepan and cover with water. Add remaining ingredients and steam on medium heat, covered, for 5 minutes. Remove lid and steam until carrots are tender and semi-dry. SERVES 6

Mixed Vegetable Smoor

Use any vegetables which are in season – especially good are carrots, beans, peas, corn kernels and potatoes.

60 g (¼ cup) butter
2 baby leeks, sliced in rounds
500 g mixed vegetables, diced
a pinch dried thyme
a pinch dried oregano
a pinch dried sweet basil

HEAT BUTTER AND stir-fry leeks until brown. Add remaining vegetables and herbs and cook quickly until just tender. Remove from heat and serve immediately. SERVES 4

Cabbage Smoor

30 ml (2 tbsp) oil
1 small onion, thinly sliced
1 small spitskop cabbage (curly top), shredded
2,5 ml (½ tsp) medium-coarse salt
2,5 ml (½ tsp) crushed chillies
5 ml (1 tsp) white sugar
a pinch turmeric
2,5 ml (½ tsp) caraway seeds

HEAT OIL IN a skillet or pan and stir-fry onion until golden-brown. Add remaining ingredients and stir-fry until just tender – be careful not to overcook. Remove from heat and serve immediately. SERVES 4

Baked Pumpkin

Serve with your favourite roast.

1 kg pumpkin, peeled and cut into thick slices
15 ml (1 tbsp) melted butter
15 ml (1 tbsp) soft brown sugar
15 ml (1 tbsp) ground cinnamon

PLACE PUMPKIN ON a well-greased baking sheet, pour over butter and sprinkle over sugar and cinnamon. Bake on middle shelf at 180 °C for 25 minutes. SERVES 6

BELOW   Green Bean Smoor, Masala Chips and Stewed Sweet Potaotes, page 57

Masala Chips

Liven up potato chips with a tang of masala and turmeric.

500 g medium potatoes, peeled and
cut into paper-thin rounds
a pinch coarse salt
a pinch leaf masala
a pinch turmeric
oil for deep-frying

SEASON POTATO ROUNDS with salt, masala and turmeric and leave to stand for a few minutes.

Deep-fry in hot oil until golden-brown and serve immediately with your favourite fish dish. SERVES 4

Stewed Sweet Potatoes

The combination of the sweet potatoes, coconut and cinnamon make this a traditional Malay side dish. Buy borrie sweet potatoes (with the red skin) if you can – they are sweeter and less watery than white-skinned sweet potatoes.

1 kg borrie sweet potatoes, peeled
and cut into thick rounds
250 ml (1 cup) water
60 ml (¼ cup) desiccated coconut
250 ml (1 cup) yellow sugar
60 g (¼ cup) butter
4 pieces stick cinnamon

TOSS THE SWEET potatoes into cold, salted water to prevent discoloration. Drain and set aside.

Heat a heavy-based saucepan over low heat and add water. When hot, add the drained sweet potatoes, coconut, sugar, butter and cinnamon. Cover and cook for about 20 minutes – do not stir.

Uncover pan and cook for a further 20 minutes until potatoes are soft. If necessary, add more sugar to taste. Stir only once or twice.

Serve immediately while still piping hot. SERVES 6

Green Bean Smoor

The word 'smoor' means 'braised' – the Malays' favourite way of preparing vegetables by braising them in oil or fat.

15 ml (1 tbsp) oil
2 baby leeks, sliced in rounds
1 x 410 g tin stubbed green beans,
drained
2,5 ml (½ tsp) medium-coarse salt
2,5 ml (½ tsp) crushed chillies
5 ml (1 tsp) white sugar
a pinch ground jeera (cumin)

HEAT OIL AND stir-fry leeks until brown. Add remaining ingredients and cook quickly until just tender. Remove from heat and serve immediately. SERVES 4

Beetroot and Onion Salad

A favourite Cape Malay salad – we eat it nearly every day.

1 bunch baby beetroot
7,5 ml (1½ tsp) salt
1 large onion, thinly sliced
2,5 ml (½ tsp) ground black pepper
or 1 piece green chilli, chopped
7,5 ml (1½ tsp) sugar
60 ml (4 tbsp) brown vinegar

CHOP OFF BEETROOT stalks. Boil beetroot covered in water until soft. This could be quite a lengthy process if you don't have a pressure cooker, so make sure you do it ahead of time. Allow to cool, then peel and slice beetroot thinly.

Add salt to onion and squeeze in one hand a few times. Toss into boiling water, stir briefly, strain and add to beetroot. Add pepper or chilli and sugar. Pour vinegar over.

This salad can be made a couple of hours in advance and refrigerated or served straight away. It looks best served in a pretty glass bowl. SERVES 4

September Cress

A winter salad – watercress and kumquats are normally only available at this time.

1 queen pineapple, peeled and grated
4 young carrots, peeled and grated
125 g (½ cups) small noodles, cooked
and drained
1 young lettuce, torn
½ bunch young watercress leaves
500 g kumquats, pitted
few stubs celery stalk and leaves
10 Californian nuts, halved
15 ml (1 tbsp) mayonnaise

COMBINE THE GRATED PINEAPPLE and carrots and leave to stand for 20 minutes. Add remaining ingredients and mix well. Chill for 30 minutes before serving. SERVES 4

Cucumber Salad

Another favourite salad in our house, often served with our Sunday meal. It's a cool companion to bredies and stews.

1 medium cucumber
125 ml (½ cup) brown vinegar
1 green chilli, sliced
sugar to taste

CUT OFF CUCUMBER ends and rub these against either end of the cucumber to prevent bitterness. Peel and run fork tines lengthwise down cucumber, then slice thinly.

Place in a bowl and add vinegar, chilli and sugar to taste. Chill before serving. SERVES 4

Sultan's Coleslaw

A coleslaw fit for a sultan!

front end of a small spitskop
cabbage (curly top)
1 x 225 g tin peach slices, halved and
drained (syrup retained)
30 ml (2 tbsp) mayonnaise
3 slices red or green pepper,
finely chopped
1 x 225 g tin choice peas, drained
125 ml (1/2 cup) whole-kernel corn,
drained
6 macadamia nuts, blanched,
peeled and quartered

SHRED, BLANCH AND drain cabbage.
Refresh in refrigerator for 30 minutes. Mix peach syrup, mayonnaise
and chopped peppers together. Add
cabbage and remaining ingredients
and allow to steep and chill for about
20 minutes before serving. SERVES 6

Feta Cheese and Gherkin Salad

4 crisp lettuce leaves, torn
1 small jar baby gherkins, drained
10 black olives
6 yellow cocktail onions
1 small onion, thinly sliced into rings
1/2 English cucumber, thinly sliced
1 firm avocado, peeled,
cut into wedges and dipped into juice
of 1 lemon
1 firm tomato, cut into wedges
10 Californian nuts, shelled and
halved

GARNISH
10 blocks feta cheese
60 ml (1/4 cup) mung bean sprouts
ground black pepper to taste

ARRANGE LETTUCE IN a shallow
bowl. Mix remaining ingredients
and pile onto lettuce leaves. Garnish
with feta cheese, sprouts and pepper.
Chill for about 20 minutes and serve.
SERVES 4-6

Tuna Salad

*You could serve this with Quick Onion Bread
(page 90) or toast for an easy
supper or a light lunch.*

3 slices English cucumber, chopped
1 small fresh tomato, cubed
2,5 ml (1/2 tsp) masala
125 ml (1/2 cup) wheat rice
(stampkoring), cooked for
30 minutes and strained
1 leek, chopped
2,5 ml (1/2 tsp) ground black pepper
30 ml (2 tbsp) mayonnaise
3 young lettuce leaves, shredded
2 x 185 g tins light meat tuna, drained

MIX ALL INGREDIENTS together
lightly except lettuce and tuna. Line
a deep glass bowl with lettuce
leaves. Arrange the salad and tuna
on the lettuce leaves and chill before
serving. SERVES 6

Crayfish Salad

*Reserve this elegant starter for special
occasions. Or serve at a brunch
as a mystery ball, wrapped in young
lettuce leaves, held together
with toothpicks.*

2 crayfish tails
a pinch cayenne pepper
15 ml (1 tbsp) mayonnaise
1 slice red pepper, chopped
3 drops lemon juice
2,5 ml (1/2 tsp) white pepper
4-6 lettuce leaves
tiny mint leaves for garnish

STEAM CRAYFISH TAILS in salted
water for 20 minutes and chill for
1 hour. Shred and toss into glass
bowl. Add cayenne pepper and
leave to stand for about 3 minutes.
Now add mayonnaise, peppers and
lemon juice.
 Arrange lettuce leaves in bowls,
spoon in crayfish mixture, and
decorate with mint leaves.
SERVES 4 AS A STARTER OR 2 AS A MEAL

Baked Bean Salad

Perfect for those in a hurry!

1 x 410 g tin baked beans, juice retained
2 baby leeks *or* spring onions
10 ml (2 tsp) chopped green pepper
3 slices English cucumber
10 ml (2 tsp) chopped parsley
10 ml (2 tsp) brown vinegar
sugar to taste

MIX ALL INGREDIENTS together,
adding sugar to taste. Chill for about
30 minutes before serving. SERVES 4

Tomato and Dhania Salad

A salad for the adventurous eater!

1 large onion, sliced
3 firm tomatoes, cut into cubes
1 small green chilli, chopped
60 ml (1/4 cup) chopped green dhania
(coriander) leaves
125 ml (1/4 cup) vinegar
sugar to taste

RUB SLICED ONION with a little salt,
toss in boiling water, strain and
squeeze dry – this prevents bitterness. Mix all the ingredients together
with sugar to taste. Chill and serve.
SERVES 4

Chilled Shrimp Salad

1 x 454 g packet peeled shrimps
a pinch cayenne pepper
60 ml (1/4 cup) mayonnaise
1 x 130 g jar white cocktail onions,
drained
very young lettuce leaves

COOK SHRIMPS ACCORDING to the
instructions on packet. Lightly mix
shrimps, pepper, mayonnaise and
onions together. Arrange lettuce
leaves in a shallow bowl. Place scoops
of shrimp mixture onto each leaf.
SERVES 4-6

Sultan's Coleslaw, page 58

Sambals, Atjars and Sauces

A sambal consists of grated vegetables or fruit, seasoned with salt, chillies or vinegar. An atjar is a relish made from sliced vegetables or fruit, flavoured with spices and covered with vinegar or oil.

Apple and Root Ginger Sambal

This has a very strong flavour – you'll only need a small amount with your bredie or stew. If preferred, leave out the chilli for a milder but still tasty sambal.

2 soft apples, peeled, cored and grated
a pinch salt
60 g (¼ cup) fresh ginger, crushed
1 clove garlic, crushed
1 green chilli, crushed
juice of 1 lemon
sugar to taste (optional)

ADD SALT TO apples and leave a while before draining.

Add the ginger, the garlic and the chilli (if using), squeezing the lemon juice over last, and add sugar to taste, if desired.

Apple Sambal

I pity those on diet – once you start eating this with your curry, you won't be able to stop!

2 hard apples, peeled and grated
juice of 1 lemon
1 clove garlic, crushed
1 small green chilli, chopped
sugar to taste (optional)

TOSS THE GRATED apple in the lemon juice, then add remaining ingredients. If the apples are sour, add a little sugar. Chill and serve.

> ### N O T E
> ✔ Sambals should be eaten straight away Atjars can be stored in airtight jars indefinately. Unless indicated, all these recipes serve 4-6 people.

Carrot and Chilli Sambal

The carrots make this sambal fairly juicy.

3 young carrots, peeled and grated
a pinch salt
1 green chilli, chopped
2,5 ml (½ tsp) sugar
15 ml (1 tbsp) black currants
sugar to taste (optional)

SPRINKLE A LITTLE salt over the grated carrots and drain after a while. Add the remaining ingredients plus sugar to taste, if desired, chill for a few minutes, then serve immediately.

OPPOSITE   Chilli Sauce (top left), page 65, Piccalilli (top right), page 64, and Lemon and Brinjal Atjar, page 65

Carrot and Pineapple Sambal

A cool and refreshing sambal, the perfect accompaniment to a hot meal.

4 carrots, peeled and
coarsely grated
1/2 pineapple, peeled and grated
15 ml (1 tbsp) blackcurrants
a few almonds, quartered
5 ml (1 tsp) sugar

MIX ALL INGREDIENTS together. Allow to stand for 30 minutes and, if preferred, drain away some of the juice so that it is almost dry.

Quince Sambal

This is a traditional recipe. The quince may change colour after about an hour of preparing this, but don't be put off – it'll still taste lovely!

1 quince, peeled, cored and grated
a pinch salt
1 green chilli, chopped *or*
a pinch cayenne pepper
juice of 1/2 lemon
sugar to taste

ADD SALT TO the grated quince and leave to stand for a while. Drain well, then add remaining ingredients with sugar to taste. Chill for a few minutes before serving.

Dhania Sambal

1 bunch green dhania (coriander) leaves
1/2 green pepper, chopped
2 green chillies, chopped
2 cloves garlic, crushed
a pinch medium-coarse salt
juice of 1 lemon
sugar to taste (optional)

WASH DHANIA LEAVES under cold, running water, and chop coarsely. Add the remaining ingredients plus sugar to taste, if desired, and serve.

Tomato and Mint Sambal

Mint leaves have a very strong flavour so remember to chop them finely.

2 firm tomatoes, diced
4 fresh mint leaves, finely chopped
1 green chilli, chopped
30 ml (2 tbsp) vinegar
sugar to taste

MIX ALL INGREDIENTS together, adding sugar to taste. Chill and serve.

Carrot and Quince Sambal

A must with curried dishes and good with fish.

1 ripe quince, peeled, cored and
coarsely grated
a pinch salt
2 young carrots, peeled and
finely grated
juice of 1/2 lemon
5 ml (1 tsp) sugar

ADD SALT TO quince and leave to stand for a good while. Press out all the liquid, place in a bowl and add remaining ingredients.

Apple and Dhania Sambal

One of my favourites!

2 Golden Delicious apples, peeled,
cored and grated
juice of 1 lemon
a pinch salt
2 cloves garlic, crushed
30 ml (2 tbsp) green dhania
(coriander) leaves
1 green chilli, chopped
sugar to taste (optional)

SOAK APPLES IN the lemon juice for a while. Chop dhania leaves coarsely and add to apples, together with remaining ingredients. If desired, add sugar to taste.

Kiwi Sambal

A fruity sambal with a refreshing taste.

4 kiwi fruit, peeled and pulped
1 clove garlic, crushed
10 ml (2 tsp) lemon juice
sugar to taste

MIX ALL INGREDIENTS together, adding sugar to taste. Chill and serve.

Cabbage, Carrot and Bean Atjar

As you use the atjar and the oil runs low, add extra oil to cover the vegetables.

15 ml (1 tbsp) methi soaked for
2 hours in boiling water
1 small spitskop cabbage (curly top),
shredded after discarding thick stalks
500 g baby carrots, peeled
and stubbed
1 x 410 g tin stubbed green beans,
drained
750 ml (3 cups) oil
7,5 ml (11/2 tsp) medium-coarse salt
10 ml (2 tsp) mustard seeds
10 ml (2 tsp) brown sugar
5 ml (1 tsp) gharum masala
5 ml (1 tsp) cayenne pepper
1 starseed petal (star anise)

POUR METHI INTO a fine sieve and rinse, drain, then add to very little boiling water and boil for 5 minutes; strain and allow to cool.

Wash cabbage and carrots in colander under cold water. Transfer to saucepan of 750 ml (3 cups) boiling salted water. Slow-steam in water for 5 minutes. Remove from heat and drain. Transfer to a large, shallow porcelain dish and allow to cool before adding green beans.

Heat oil and add the spices. Stir a few times, maintaining a low heat. Remove from heat and allow to cool. Add to vegetables, so that they are completely covered with oil; allow to draw in the fridge for a few days. Bottle and store in the fridge.

Kiwi Sambal and Tomato and Mint Sambal, page 62

Lemon and Kumquat Atjar

A fresh-tasting, all-round atjar, ideal with a breyani or curry.

10 ml (2 tsp) methi, soaked for
2 hours in boiling water
500 g lemons, quartered and pitted
2,5 ml (½ tsp) salt
500 g kumquats, pitted and cut
into wedges
750 ml (3 cups) oil
10 ml (2 tsp) turmeric
10 ml (2 tsp) tandoori masala
5 ml (1 tsp) gharum masala
1 starseed petal (star anise)

POUR METHI INTO a fine sieve and rinse, drain, then add to very little boiling water and boil for 5 minutes; strain and allow to cool.

Steam the lemons for 5 minutes in a little water with the salt. Drain and set aside. Pour boiling water over the kumquats and steam for 2 minutes. Drain and add to lemons.

Heat the oil to just before boiling point and add spices. Remove from heat and allow to cool completely. Pour over lemons and kumquats and store in an airtight jar in the fridge.

Apricot and Peach Chutney

A fruity chutney always goes well with a bredie or stew.

30 ml (2 tbsp) coriander seeds
10 ml (2 tsp) oil
1 medium onion, chopped
750 ml (3 cups) brown vinegar
1 x 450 g tin apricot jam
1 x 450 g tin peach jam
125 ml (½ cup) sugar
15 ml (1 tbsp) dried, crushed chilli
250 ml (1 cup) prepared fruit chutney
15 ml (1 tbsp) crushed garlic
5 ml (1 tsp) salt
1 starseed petal (star anise)

SCORCH CORIANDER SEEDS in 5 ml (1 tsp) oil in a heavy-based pan and remove from the heat the moment they change colour. Grind in a mill or crush with a rolling pin and set aside. Scorch onion in 5 ml (1 tsp) oil and add to coriander.

Heat 375 ml (1½ cups) vinegar over low heat. Add jams to the remaining vinegar and stir well, using a wooden spoon.

Add the remaining ingredients, including onion mixture, to this and stir. Pour mixture into warm vinegar and bring to the boil, stirring occasionally. Set aside to cool, then bottle and refrigerate. MAKES ABOUT 1¼ LITRES (5 CUPS)

Piccalilli

My prize recipe – not even my children know how to make this! It's a real success at a bazaar if made the right way. Delight your family and serve alongside corned beef and roasts.

2 bunches carrots, peeled
1 medium cauliflower
2 x 410 g tins sliced green beans, drained
1 small jar gherkins, drained and thickly sliced
50 ml (3 tbsp) dry mustard
10 ml (2 tsp) cayenne pepper
10 ml (2 tsp) turmeric
30 ml (2 tbsp) oil
750 ml (3 cups) cold water
5 ml (1 tsp) salt
3 x 750 ml bottles white vinegar
60 ml (1/4 cup) cornflour
15 ml (1 tbsp) mustard seeds
1 starseed petal (star anise)
625 ml (2 1/2 cups) sugar

CUT CARROTS INTO stubs. Pour boiling water over and steam for 5 minutes. Drain and transfer to basin. Prepare cauliflower in the same manner, but do not make florets too small. Do not overcook vegetables as it will make the piccalilli soggy. Add drained green beans and gherkins.

Mix the mustard, cayenne pepper, turmeric and the oil with 375 ml (1 1/2 cups) cold water and salt. Boil vinegar and stir in the mustard paste. Make a paste from the cornflour and remaining water, and stir into the boiling vinegar mixture. Continue stirring, reduce heat and add the starseed petal and sugar. Remove from heat and when cold, pour over vegetables.

Leave to draw in the fridge for half a day, then bottle in airtight jars – it will last indefinitely in the fridge. Serve with roasts or grills or even on a sandwich with cold meats. MAKES 4-5 X 750G JARS

Piccalilli (top), this page, and Apricot and Peach Chutney (bottom), page 63

Lemon and Brinjal Atjar

One of the best-loved Muslim atjar recipes.

15 ml (1 tbsp) medium-coarse salt
6 thick-skinned lemons, wedged,
pitted and lightly squeezed
60 ml (¼ cup) methi, soaked for
2 hours in boiling water
750 ml (3 cups) oil
10 ml (2 tsp) turmeric
30 ml (2 tbsp) crushed chilli
5 ml (1 tsp) red masala
5 ml (1 tsp) gharum masala
1 starseed petal (star anise)
10 ml (2 tsp) sugar
600 g baby brinjals, wedged and
soaked in salt water
500 ml (2 cups) boiling water

SPRINKLE 7,5 ML (1½ TSP) salt over the lemon wedges and leave to stand overnight. Pour boiling water over the lemons, set aside for 30 minutes, then rinse and drain.

Pour methi into a fine sieve and rinse, drain, then add to very little boiling water and boil for 5 minutes; strain and allow to cool.

In a heavy-based saucepan heat oil to almost boiling point, remove from heat, add methi, 5 ml (1 tsp) salt, 7,5 ml (1½ tsp) turmeric, chilli, remaining spices, and sugar. Stir well and set aside.

Add brinjal wedges to remaining 2,5 ml (½ tsp) turmeric, the boiling water and remaining 2,5 ml (½ tsp) salt. Cook rapidly for 5 minutes, then slowly for 10 minutes. Remove from heat, drain and allow to cool.

Layer the lemons and brinjals in a large dish. Add the hot oil and spice mixture to it, cover and allow to draw in the fridge for three days. Bottle in airtight jars and store in the fridge.

Pineapple and Peach Mayonnaise

A real winner – serve as a relish with roasts or grills.

1 x 385 g tin peaches in thick syrup,
drained (syrup retained)
1 medium pineapple, peeled,
then grated or chopped
200 g (1 cup) small noodles, cooked
1 x 250 g jar mayonnaise
3 slices red pepper, finely chopped

CUBE OR CUT peaches into strips and place in a mixing bowl. Add pineapple, noodles and mayonnaise. Now gently blend in peach syrup and stir lightly.

Garnish with the chopped peppers. Serve with a roast or with Devilled Chicken (page 25) or Potroast Leg of Lamb (page 28).

Malayan Relish

A colourful and tangy sauce that goes especially well with curries.

3 firm tomatoes
6 mint leaves, chopped
a pinch salt
a pinch paprika
1 baby onion, chopped
15 ml (1 tbsp) sugar

BLANCH, PEEL AND pulp the tomatoes. Combine with the remaining ingredients, mix thoroughly and serve straight away.

NOTES

✔ Tinned apricots can be used instead of peaches when making Pineapple and Peach Mayonnaise (recipe above).
✔ Atjars should be stored in airtight jars in the fridge.
✔ If using green dhania (coriander) leaves instead of mint, use double the amount.
✔ A dried orange peel in the teapot gives a delicious flavour when making tea.

Chilli Sauce

Fiery stuff – unless you're tough, have a glass of water close at hand!

1 x 410 g tin tomato purée
45 ml (3 tbsp) crushed, dried chilli
1 x 65 g tin tomato paste
15 ml (1 tbsp) oil
30 ml (2 tbsp) white sugar, or to taste

MIX ALL INGREDIENTS together, adding sugar to taste. It can be served immediately but will last indefinitely in an airtight jar stored in the fridge.

Cream of Mushroom Sauce

A lovely accompaniment to roasts and grills.

5 ml (1 tsp) cake flour
500 ml (2 cups) milk or thin cream
15 ml (1 tsp) melted butter
a pinch salt
a pinch pepper
1 x 250 g tin button mushrooms,
drained and halved

MAKE A PASTE with the flour and milk by slowly cooking milk over medium heat and stirring in the flour. Add remaining ingredients, stirring in the mushrooms last. Serve immediately while hot.

Tartar Sauce

A must with grilled or fried fish.

3 slices red or green
pepper, chopped
30 ml (2 tbsp) olives, chopped
a pinch paprika
250 ml (1 cup) mayonnaise
juice of 1 lemon
1 small onion, finely chopped

MIX ALL THE ingredients together and chill for a few minutes in the fridge. Serve immediately.

Cooking for Large Numbers

Religious ceremonies, weddings, births and funerals – these form an important part of the Malay calendar where family, friends and neighbours feast together, so it's essential that we know how to cater for large groups.

Smoked Mussel and Baby Clam Curry

This queen of shellfish dishes can be served as a delicious starter and takes only 20 minutes to prepare.

250 ml (1 cup) boiling water
30 g (2 tbsp) tamarind
10 ml (2 tsp) sugar
125 ml (1/2 cup) oil
1 large onion, chopped
1 small tomato, blanched, peeled and pulped
10 ml (2 tsp) tomato sauce
5 ml (1 tsp) turmeric
5 ml (1 tsp) red leaf masala
1 cardamom pod
2 pieces stick cinnamon
375 ml (1 1/2 cups) water
3 x 290 g tin baby clams, drained
1 x 525 g tin smoked mussels in cottonseed oil
1/4 green pepper, chopped
2,5 ml (1/2 tsp) medium-coarse salt
5 ml (1 tsp) garlic and ginger paste
a pinch jeera (cumin) seeds *or* ground jeera
10 curry leaves with stalks

POUR BOILING WATER onto tamarind, add sugar, stir and set aside.

Heat oil in a heavy-based saucepan on high heat. Toss in onion and brown a little. Stir once or twice, then add tomato pulp and sauce, turmeric, masala, cardamom, cinnamon and water. Reduce heat to low.

Drain tamarind through a sieve into a saucepan. Gently add baby clams, mussels and remaining ingredients. Stir to heat through.

Serve immediately in small bowls lined with lettuce leaves, cocktail rolls on the side, or serve on a bed of fluffy white rice. SERVES 15 PEOPLE AS A STARTER

Bulk Rice

2 kg uncooked long-grain white rice
4 litres (12 cups) boiling water
100 g (1/2 cup) medium-coarse salt
2 cloves
2 small leeks, finely chopped
30 ml (2 tbsp) oil
2,5 ml (1/2 tsp) turmeric
30 ml (2 tbsp) butter

USE TWO SAUCEPANS to cook in and divide all the ingredients in half. Cook the rice in the boiling water in the two pans with remaining ingredients, except the butter, for about 25 minutes or until tender. Drain and fast-steam the rice in colanders with the butter until hot. SERVES 20

OPPOSITE Mutton Curry, page 70, Lemon and Brinjal Atjar, page 65, and Malay Roti, page 92

Labarang Oven Frikkadels

An all-time favourite which is often served at weddings and other joyous occasions.

3 kg coarse steak mince
2 loaves stale white bread, sliced, soaked in water for 5 minutes and squeezed dry
500 ml (2 cups) cold water
2 large onions, chopped
4 large eggs
25 ml (1½ tbsp) medium-coarse salt
½ bunch parsley, chopped
20 mint leaves, finely chopped
7,5 ml (1½ tsp) ground nutmeg
15 ml (1 tbsp) ground black pepper
4 green chillies, chopped
½ small red *or* green pepper, chopped
7,5 ml (1½ tsp) turmeric
10 ml (2 tsp) red masala
250 g (1 cup) soft butter
1 firm tomato, diced

WASH MINCE IN a colander or sieve under slow-running cold water. Drain well, then combine mince and bread and mix well in a large basin.

Add remaining ingredients, except tomato. Using both hands, work very lightly and slowly, making sure that everything is blended thoroughly. Now add tomato.

Shape into frikkadels or spread mixture evenly in a large baking sheet and cut into squares when done. Bake on middle shelf of oven at 180 °C for 30-40 minutes, depending on size of frikkadels or the height of the mixture on the baking sheet.

Serve with mashed potato, peas, and Beetroot and Onion Salad (page 57). MAKES 86 FRIKKADELS

Masala and Garlic Chicken

It's such a delicious meal that you'll be surprised how easy it is to make.

2 x 1 kg chickens
a few slices red *or* green pepper
20 ml (1½ tbsp) medium-coarse salt
3 cloves garlic, crushed
30 ml (2 tbsp) red, roasted masala
30 ml (2 tbsp) peri-peri oil
1 kg new potatoes
oil for deep-frying

RUB THE CHICKEN skin with red or green pepper. Then salt chicken all over and set aside for a few minutes. Mix garlic, masala and peri-peri oil in a saucer, rub into chicken and marinate for 30 minutes.

Transfer to a roasting pan. Grill on middle shelf for 1 hour at 200 °C, basting occasionally with the cooking juices until chicken is tender.

Deep-fry whole potatoes in hot oil and serve alongside chicken with Beetroot and Onion Salad (page 57) and Sweet Sultana Yellow Rice (page 54). SERVES 10

Labarang Kabobs

These oblong frikkadels consist of hard-boiled eggs wrapped in mince and fried – they are usually served at Eidul-Fitr (Labarang).

6 slices stale bread, soaked in water for 5 minutes and squeezed dry
1 kg coarse steak mince
1 onion, chopped
1 tomato, blanched, peeled and pulped
1 egg
60 ml (¼ cup) chopped parsley
2,5 ml (½ tsp) ground nutmeg
7,5 ml (1½ tsp) salt
5 ml (1 tsp) pepper
6 cloves garlic, crushed
136 g (½ cup) butter *or* margarine
10 hard-boiled eggs, halved lengthwise
oil for frying

MIX ALL INGREDIENTS together except hard-boiled eggs and oil. If the mixture is still too stiff, add a little water. Form into ovals and put half a hard-boiled egg into each kebab. Fry in very warm oil until done and serve with yellow rice and salads. MAKES 20

NOTES

✔ One small chilli, chopped, or a pinch of cayenne pepper can be added to give the Sosati Curry more bite. Serve with Cinnamon Rice (page 54).
✔ A pressure cooker will cook your food in half the time of that of an ordinary saucepan.
✔ Heat the stove plate before placing your pot on it. This will save you cooking time and electricity.
✔ The Labarang Kabobs can be oven-fried or lightly pan-fried.
✔ When bulk cooking, first lightly braise the onions, then add the meat which must be well drained, otherwise it will shred.
✔ Chicken dishes should always be cooked on medium heat.

Sosati Curry

When catering for a large Sunday party, this is a choice meal to serve.

125 ml (½ cup) boiling water
90 g (¾ cup) tamarind
10 ml (2 tsp) sugar
2 kg lamb cutlets
1 large onion, chopped
10 ml (2 tsp) medium-coarse salt
1 slice red *or* green pepper
10 cloves garlic, crushed
6 allspice
4 cardamom pods
2 bay leaves
2 whole cloves
5 ml (1 tsp) turmeric
10 ml (2 tsp) red roasted masala
250 ml (1 cup) cold water
15 ml (1 tbsp) oil
10 ml (2 tsp) fine, dry breadcrumbs

POUR BOILING WATER over tamarind and sugar and leave to soak in boiling water for a few minutes. Drain and set aside.

Over medium heat, arrange cutlets on the base of a saucepan, top with onion, salt and the remaining ingredients, except the tamarind, water, oil and breadcrumbs. Braise until well browned.

Add cold water and oil, cover and cook for 30 minutes. Uncover and allow to brown a little. Reduce heat, adding extra cold water in very small quantities if necessary. Simmer for a further 30 minutes. Finally add tamarind pulp and liquid and breadcrumbs. This is a semi-dry meal so the sauce should not be too runny.

Serve with boiled potatoes and saffron rice. Two drops of egg yellow food colouring can be substituted for saffron and 2 pieces stick cinnamon make the rice sweeter. SERVES 18

Vegetable Mutton Curry

A fairly expensive meal, so save it for when your relatives are visiting on the weekend.

60 ml (¼ cup) oil
3 pieces stick cinnamon
2 large onions, chopped
1 kg thin lamb ribs
500 g mutton knuckles
500 ml (2 cups) water
1 kg lamb leg chops, cubed
10 ml (2 tsp) tomato sauce
1 small tomato, blanched, peeled and pulped
6 thin slices green pepper
1 small spitskop cabbage (curly top), shredded
1 bunch young carrots, peeled and cut into rounds
5 ml (1 tsp) turmeric
5 ml (1 tsp) leaf masala
5 ml (1 tsp) garlic and ginger paste
500 g new potatoes
1 bunch young turnips, peeled and sliced
5 ml (1 tsp) sugar
10 ml (2 tsp) medium-coarse salt
2 starseed petals (star anise)
6 curry leaves
2,5 ml (½ tsp) ground jeera (cumin)

HEAT OIL IN a large heavy-based saucepan over medium heat. Add cinnamon and onion and brown. Stir, then add ribs and knuckles and cook for 20 minutes in 375 ml (1½ cups) water. Now add cubed chops and simmer for another 20 minutes. Braise once, then add remaining 125 ml (½ cup) water.

Add remaining ingredients, except jeera. Stir thoroughly and simmer slowly over low heat until almost done. Finally add jeera. SERVES 14

BELOW Labarang Kabobs, page 68, and Sweet Sultana Yellow Rice, page 54

Smoked Mussel and Baby Clam Curry, page 66

Mutton Curry

*A mouth-watering curry with
plenty of thick gravy,
traditionally served at weddings
with rice or roti.*

250 ml (1 cup) oil
5 pieces stick cinnamon
6 cardamom pods, slightly cracked
4 large onions, chopped
10 ml (2 tsp) turmeric
10 ml (2 tsp) leaf masala
2 ripe tomatoes, blanched, peeled
and pulped
15 ml (1 tbsp) tomato sauce
1 kg lamb hindquarter, cubed
2 kg lamb leg chops, cubed
1 kg shoulder of mutton, cubed
20 ml (1½ tbsp) medium-coarse salt
500 ml (2 cups) water
2 kg small potatoes, peeled
and halved
10 cloves garlic, crushed
15 ml (1 tbsp) crushed fresh ginger
1 green pepper, chopped
40 ml (2½ tbsp) gharum masala *or*
jeera (cumin) seeds or powder
2 starseed petals (star anise)
10 ml (2 tsp) fine, dry breadcrumbs
5 ml (1 tsp) sugar
125 ml (½ cup) chopped green
dhania (coriander) leaves

HEAT OIL, CINNAMON and carda-
mon in a saucepan over medium
heat. Add onion and brown before
adding turmeric, masala, tomato
and tomato sauce. Stir well, then
add cubed meat and salt. Cook,
covered, for 20 minutes, braising
once and stirring thoroughly.

Add water and cook, still covered,
until meat is tender. Now add potatoes and remaining ingredients with
a very little water if necessary.
Reduce heat. Stir thoroughly once
or twice and simmer until potatoes
are cooked.

Serve this meal with Cinnamon
Pumpkin (page 52) Lemon and
Brinjal Atjar (page 64) and Bulk
Rice (page 66) or roti. SERVES 24

Mince and Vegetable Breyani

The meat, vegetables and rice are served in one pot – a good meal for a large group.

125 ml (½ cup) oil
4 pieces stick cinnamon
1 large onion, chopped
10 ml (2 tsp) tomato sauce
1 small tomato, blanched, peeled and pulped
1 cauliflower, broken into florets
6 carrots, peeled and stubbed
375 ml (1½ cups) water
7,5 ml (1½ tsp) leaf masala
5 ml (1 tsp) turmeric
½ spitskop cabbage (curly top), shredded
10 ml (2 tsp) medium-coarse salt
1,5 kg coarse steak mince
1 x 410 g tin whole kernel corn
10 ml (2 tsp) garlic, crushed
10 ml (2 tsp) ginger paste
500 g frozen green beans
5 ml (1 tsp) gharum masala

RICE
700 g (3½ cups) uncooked long-grain white rice
1 litre (4 cups) boiling water
10 ml (2 tsp) salt
2 pieces stick cinnamon
4 cardamom pods
5 ml (1 tsp) turmeric

HEAT OIL AND cinnamon together over medium heat. Toss in onion and brown, then add tomato sauce and tomato pulp. Stir briefly, then add cauliflower, carrots and 250 ml (1 cup) cold water. Steam for 10 minutes.

Now add masala, turmeric, cabbage and salt with 125 ml (½ cup) water and steam for a further 5 minutes. Add mince and remaining ingredients, except gharum masala. Stir thoroughly and simmer, uncovered. Water can be added after about 15 minutes if necessary. The saucepan must be almost dry. Stir, remove from heat and add beans.

Now cook rice in boiling water with salt, cinnamon, cardamom and turmeric. Drain, strain and steam in a colander over rapidly boiling water for 10 minutes. Allow to cool. Mix breyani mixture and rice together, then sprinkle gharum masala lightly over breyani. Cover saucepan and steam for a further 10 minutes over low heat.

Serve with Lemon and Kumquat Atjar (page 63) or Apple Sambal (page 60). SERVES 20

Old Cape Denningvleis

Denningvleis is meat flavoured with bay leaves and tamarind, vinegar or lemon juice. The word 'denning' originated from the Javanese 'dendeng', the meat of the water buffalo – but nowadays we use mutton!

375 ml (1½ cups) oil
2 kg mutton shoulder
2 kg mutton cutlets
2 kg thick mutton ribs
1 kg onions, chopped
2 whole heads of garlic, crushed
30 ml (2 tbsp) medium-coarse salt
20 ml (1½ tbsp) ground black pepper
10 whole cloves
25 allspice
20 bay leaves
7,5 ml (1½ tsp) ground nutmeg
250 g (1 cup) tamarind
500 ml (2 cups) boiling water
10 ml (2 tsp) sugar
2 large green peppers, chopped
45 ml (3 tbsp) fine, dry breadcrumbs

MASHED POTATO
6 kg small potatoes, peeled and halved
15 ml (1 tbsp) baking powder
1,5 litres (6 cups) milk
5 ml (1 tsp) ground nutmeg

HEAT OIL IN a large catering saucepan over medium heat. Cut meat into suitably-size pieces and spread on base of saucepan. Add onion, spices and remaining ingredients, except tamarind, boiling water, sugar, peppers and breadcrumbs. Cover saucepan and braise meat until tender, adding small amounts of water to the saucepan.

Meanwhile soak tamarind and sugar in boiling water for a few minutes, drain and set aside. When the meat is braised and well browned, add peppers and tamarind pulp and liquid (remove pips) to saucepan. Denning stew should not be too saucy. To thicken the sauce, add breadcrumbs when the cooking is done, 5 minutes before serving.

Boil potatoes until soft, then mash with baking powder, milk and nutmeg. Serve stew with mashed potatoes and Glazed Carrots (page 55). SERVES 40

Peri-Peri Chicken

The peri-peri oil makes the chicken succulent and adds a lively tang to the dish.

4 medium chickens, cut into portions
30 ml (2 tbsp) medium-coarse salt
15 ml (1 tbsp) red masala
60 ml (¼ cup) peri-peri oil
15 ml (1 tbsp) ground cinnamon
125 g (½ cup) margarine
10 pieces stick cinnamon
250 ml (1 cup) water

CLEAN CHICKEN WELL. Mix salt, masala, peri-peri oil and ground cinnamon together, rub into chicken and leave to stand for 1 hour.

Melt margarine over medium heat in a catering saucepan. Add chicken with cinnamon sticks and cook quickly until chicken is browned. Add water and cook until tender, then grill until the chicken is crisp and golden-brown. Serve with potato chips or rice. SERVES 20

Puddings

Partial to puddings, the traditional Malay favours desserts which are usually baked. Lighter, fresher fridge desserts with fruit as the base are lavishly decorated with cream, cherries and chocolate vermicilli.

Vinegar Pudding

Some people call this malva pudding – it's such a 'lekker' pudding that you won't be able to stop eating until it's finished!

75 g (5 tbsp) soft butter
185 ml (³/4 cup) soft brown sugar
2 eggs, beaten
15 ml (1 tbsp) apricot jam
15 ml (1 tbsp) vinegar
375 ml (1¹/2 cups) milk
a pinch salt
4 x 250 ml (4 cups) self-raising flour
2,5 ml (¹/2 tsp) bicarbonate
of soda

SAUCE
500 ml (2 cups) boiling water
100 g (¹/2 cup) soft butter
125 ml (¹/2 cup) soft brown sugar
5 ml (1 tsp) treacle (*see* page 78)
250 ml (1 cup) evaporated milk

CREAM BUTTER, SUGAR and eggs together, add remaining ingredients and mix well. Turn into a greased ovenproof dish and bake at 140 °C on middle shelf for 30 minutes.

To make the sauce, combine and heat ingredients together, stirring until hot. Remove from heat and pour over warm pudding. Serve topped with cream and pecan nuts, if desired. SERVES 8-10

Sago Pudding

A regular weekend pud that's quick and easy to prepare!

250 ml (1 cup) sugar
3 large eggs
5 ml (1 tsp) vanilla essence
250 ml (1 cup) sago, soaked in water
for 3 hours, then drained
a pinch salt

a pinch ground cinnamon
500 ml (2 cups) milk
a pinch ground nutmeg
90 g (¹/3 cup) butter *or* margarine,
sliced
15 ml (1 tbsp) cake flour, made into a
thin paste with a little water

CREAM SUGAR AND eggs for 2 minutes and then add vanilla essence. Stir in sago and remaining ingredients, except nutmeg, butter and flour paste, and transfer to a greased ovenproof dish.

Stir in sliced butter and flour paste and sprinkle with nutmeg. Preheat oven to 180 °C and bake pudding on middle shelf for about 30 minutes. Serve hot with stewed raisins and honey or green fig preserve syrup. SERVES 4-6

OPPOSITE   Vinegar Pudding

Baked Date Pudding

This is my favourite pudding, an olden time dessert learnt from my granny.

90 g (⅓ cup) soft butter
125 ml (½ cup) soft brown sugar
2 large eggs, beaten
250 ml (1 cup) milk
15 ml (1 tbsp) oil
a pinch salt
2,5 ml (½ tsp) ground cinnamon
2,5 ml (½ tsp) ground ginger
2,5 ml (½ tsp) ground mixed spice
4 x 250 ml (4 cups) self-raising flour
2,5 ml (½ tsp) bicarbonate of soda
1 x 250 g packet stoneless dates

CREAM BUTTER, SUGAR and egg together. Add milk, oil and salt. Mix dry ingredients together, except dates, and add to egg mixture. Finally roll dates in a little flour and add, mixing well.

Turn out into a greased ovenproof dish. Bake on middle shelf at 180 °C for 40 minutes and serve with thin custard. SERVES 6-8

Lockshen Delight

Lockshen is similar to vermicilli but thinner. You'll find it in supermarkets in the pasta section.

180 g (¾ cup) butter *or* margarine
2 x 250 g boxes lockshen
200 g (1 cup) white sugar
750 ml (3 cups) water
100 g (¾ cup) pecan *or* Brazil nuts, chipped, *or* sultanas/ seedless raisins

MELT BUTTER IN a saucepan over medium heat, add lockshen and stir continuously and vigorously until golden-brown. Add sugar and water and cover saucepan. Reduce heat to very low and simmer for 10 minutes. Stir lockshen lightly to ensure that it doesn't dry out – if it does, add a little warm water. Serve hot or cold in small bowls, decorated with nuts, sultanas or raisins. SERVES 12

Apricot Jam Baked Pudding

You can serve this hot or cold – I prefer to eat it hot.

125 g (½ cup) butter *or* margarine
250 ml (1 cup) sugar
2 eggs, beaten
10 ml (2 tsp) oil
4 x 250 ml (4 cups) self-raising flour
a pinch salt
250 ml (1 cup) milk
5 ml (1 tsp) treacle (*see* page 78)
15 ml (1 tbsp) apricot jam
2,5 ml (½ tsp) bicarbonate of soda

CREAM BUTTER AND sugar together, then add eggs. Blend well, then add oil, flour, salt, milk, treacle and jam. Stir thoroughly, add bicarbonate of soda and mix well.

Turn into a well-greased baking tin or bread tin – it mustn't be too shallow. Bake at 180 °C on middle shelf for 30 minutes. Serve hot or cold with thin custard. SERVES 6-8

Boeber

Boeber is a ceremonial drink but we also serve it as a dessert in winter – and sometimes even for breakfast!

15 ml (1 tbsp) butter
3 small cinnamon sticks
2 cardamom pods
250 ml (1 cup) lockshen, slightly crushed
125 ml (½ cup) sago, soaked for 2 hours and drained
500 ml (2 cups) boiling water
60 ml (4 tbsp) condensed milk
a pinch salt

HEAT BUTTER IN a saucepan over medium heat. When soft, stir in cinnamon, cardamom and lockshen and cook until the lockshen is light brown.

Now add sago, stir to mix, then add remaining ingredients. Cook for about 15 minutes, stirring occasionally. If left to stand, the boeber will thicken. Before serving in individual glasses or bowls, add a little milk to each portion. SERVES 4-6

Strawberry Fridge Dessert

250 g fresh strawberries, washed and hulled
30 ml (2 tbsp) white sugar
40 ml (2½ tbsp) cold water
1 extra-large egg, separated
10 ml (2 tsp) custard powder
750 ml (3 cups) hot water
2,5 ml (½ tsp) gelatine
2 x 80 g packets strawberry jelly
chocolate vermicelli for decoration

CUT STRAWBERRIES INTO uneven pieces and place them in a small saucepan. Add sugar, 30 ml (2 tbsp) cold water and simmer for 10 minutes. Meanwhile, combine egg yolk, custard powder and 10 ml (2 tsp) cold water. Stir well and add to strawberry mixture, stirring rapidly for a few minutes. Remove from heat and set aside to cool.

Allow hot water to cool a little and then stir in gelatine and jelly. Leave to cool. When cold, add strawberry mixture and blend thoroughly. Beat egg white until frothy and fold in. Pour into a glass dish. Top with chocolate vermicelli, chill and serve. Sliced strawberries and cream make a good topping too. SERVES 8-10

NOTE

✔ Chopped almonds or seedless sultanas can be added to the Boeber if desired.

Lockshen Delight, page 74

Pear Snow

Light and delicious, perfect for rounding off a hot, spicy meal.

7,5 ml (1½ tsp) gelatine
2 x 80 g packets lemon jelly
500 ml (2 cups) hot water
1 x 825 g tin pears, drained and syrup reserved
1 x 410 g tin evaporated milk, chilled overnight
50 g Peppermint Crisp, chipped
10 pecan nuts, slightly crushed

IN A LARGE bowl, combine 5 ml (1 tsp) gelatine and jelly, slowly adding the hot water. Stir well and set aside. Mash pears and set aside.

Heat pear syrup over low heat with remaining gelatine. Stir, then remove from heat and add to jelly. In a deep mixing bowl, whisk or beat evaporated milk vigorously until very stiff, add to pear mixture and then add jelly. Stir slowly until well blended. Pour into a glass bowl, decorate with the chipped chocolate and top with nuts. SERVES 8

Tameletjies

Pine kernels are very expensive – why not collect the ones that have fallen from the pine trees, like we used to? Coarse coconut dyed with food colouring of your choice can be used instead of the kernels.

500 ml (2 cups) caramel sugar
5 ml (1 tsp) honey
375 ml (1½ cups) boiling water
100 g (¾ cup) pine kernels
2,5 ml (½ tsp) cream of tartar

BEFORE YOU BEGIN, make 3 large or 6 small rectangular containers out of aluminium foil or greaseproof paper, 2 cm high x 6 cm wide x 12 cm long. In the old days, lined pages from exercise books were used. The four corners will stay together because of the stickiness of the tameletjie.

Add sugar and honey to the boiling water; bring to the boil again. Cook on low heat until sugar begins to bubble. Stir for about 2 minutes or until the syrup starts to get sticky. Remove from heat and allow to cool. Stir in the pine kernels, then add cream of tartar and mix well.

Spoon the mixture into the containers (or any shallow container) so they are three-quarters full. Leave in the fridge to set for 1 hour. MAKES 3 LARGE OR 6 SMALL CONTAINERS

Pineapple Fridge Dessert, page 77

Summer Pear Flan

You'll need special flan baking tins for this recipe.

45 ml (3 tbsp) milk
45 ml (3 tbsp) water
120 g (¹/₂ cup) butter
250 ml (1 cup) castor sugar
2 eggs, separated, whites
lightly beaten
500 ml (2 cups) cake flour
10 ml (2 tsp) baking powder
1 x 410 g tin pears in thick syrup,
drained and syrup reserved
a pinch gelatine

PLACE MILK, WATER and butter in a saucepan and bring to the boil, stirring gently. Remove from heat and set aside to cool.

When completely cool, add sugar and beat well. Now add egg yolks, then fold in egg whites and finally flour and baking powder.

Pour mixture into 2 flan baking tins which have been wiped with a few grains of salt before greasing. Bake at 180 °C for 25-30 minutes. Set aside to cool completely and turn out onto a plate when cold.

Heat pear syrup, combined with gelatine, over low heat. Stir until almost boiling. Remove from heat and cool completely. Chill a little in refrigerator and remove the moment it starts to set. Pour over flan cases and decorate with pears. Serve chilled. SERVES 6

NOTES

✔ The pears can be replaced with tinned apricots, peaches, pineapple or other fruit, if prefered.
✔ To prevent possible mouth sores from pineapple, rub pineapple lightly with salt after peeling.
✔ A few drops of lemon juice added to water before apples are placed in the pot will prevent discolouring.
✔ Always sift flour before using it.

Jam Tart

8 x 250 ml (8 cups) cake flour
750 g (3 cups) butter, chilled
5 ml (1 tsp) salt
2 eggs, separated, yolks beaten
750 ml (3 cups) iced water
10 ml (2 tsp) cream of tartar
60 ml (¹/₄ cup) cornflour
1 x 450 g tin apricot whole fruit jam
15 ml (1 tbsp) lemon juice
2 eggs, beaten with
10 ml (2 tsp) milk

SET ASIDE 60 ml (¹/₄ cup) flour for rolling out dough. Sift remaining flour and coarsely grate 250 g (1 cup) butter. Mix flour, butter, salt and egg yolks. Make a soft, firm dough by gradually adding water.

Roll out dough and spread thin slices of butter over. Add cream of tartar to cornflour. Top dough with a few sprinkles of this mix. Fold dough unevenly and roll out with a little flour rubbed onto the rolling pin. Repeat process until all the butter has been used. Cut pastry into two or three manageable pieces. Chill in fridge overnight.

Roll out pastry and line tart plates. Spread three-quarters of the jam over pastry. Bake on middle shelf for 12-15 minutes at 200 °C. When tarts are done, gloss with beaten egg. Cover with a cloth for a few minutes before removing from tins. MAKES 4 LARGE TARTS

Potato Pudding

Delicious cut into squares and decorated with stewed fruit.

500 g small potatoes, peeled
and halved
6 eggs, beaten
125 g (¹/₂ cup) butter
250 ml (1 cup) sugar
5 ml (1 tsp) salt
2 drops almond essence
5 ml (1 tsp) vanilla essence

2,5 ml (¹/₂ tsp) ground cinnamon
1 litre (4 cups) milk
15 ml (1 tbsp) cake flour, made into a
paste with 60 ml (¹/₄ cup) milk

BOIL, DRAIN AND mash potatoes. Mix all ingredients together, except milk and flour paste, using half the butter. Now add milk, flour paste and remaining butter.

Bake in a greased ovenproof dish at 180 °C on middle shelf for about 40 minutes. SERVES 10-12

Pineapple Fridge Dessert

Minneolas or apples can be substituted for the pineapple – remember to use the appropriate flavour jelly and essence for the different fruits.

1 large queen pineapple, grated
15 ml (1 tbsp) white sugar
45 ml (3 tbsp) cold water
10 ml (2 tsp) custard powder
2 eggs, separated
2,5 ml (¹/₂ tsp) gelatine
750 ml (3 cups) hot water
2 x 80 g packets pineapple jelly
a drop pineapple essence

COOK PINEAPPLE AND sugar in 30 ml (2 tbsp) water in a saucepan over medium heat for 10 minutes, stirring occasionally. In the meantime, add 15 ml (1 tbsp) cold water to custard powder and egg yolks and mix well.

Pour custard mixture into saucepan, stirring vigorously. Remove from heat and leave to cool.

Add gelatine and hot water to the jelly powder, stir, then add essence. Beat egg whites until stiff.

When everything has cooled, gently fold fruit mixture and egg whites into jelly. Mix thoroughly. Transfer to freezer for 30 minutes. Remove to refrigerator, top with well-beaten fresh cream and decorate with chopped nuts and cherries before serving. SERVES 8-10

Cakes, Tarts and Biscuits

Biscuit and cake tins are always full in case of unexpected visitors. Here I've given some of our traditional recipes, as well as some which have been adopted by our community.

Puff Pastry

15 ml (1 tbsp) cornflour
2,5 ml (½ tsp) cream of tartar
4 x 250 ml (4 cups) cake flour
375 g (1½ cups) butter, chilled
30 ml (2 tbsp) oil
juice of ½ lemon
1 egg yolk, beaten
250 ml (1 cup) iced water

MIX CORNFLOUR AND cream of tartar; set aside. Sift flour and rub in 60 g (¼ cup) of butter. Add rest of ingredients, except remaining butter, to make a pastry. Roll out pastry on a floured surface and flake pieces of butter unevenly over it. Dredge cornflour and cream of tartar mixture over; fold pastry unevenly. Roll out twice more until all butter has been used; chill for a few hours. MAKES 3 LARGE TART SHELLS

Kolwyntjies

Kolwyntjies are also known as queen cakes.

125 g (½ cup) butter
250 ml (1 cup) castor sugar
3 eggs, beaten
125 ml (½ cup) orange juice
5 ml (1 tsp) grated orange rind
4 x 250 ml (4 cups) self-raising flour
5 ml (1 tsp) baking powder
125 ml (½ cup) currants
60 ml (¼ cup) oil

CREAM BUTTER AND sugar together well, then add eggs. Now add the remaining ingredients and stir thoroughly, adding a little milk if the mixture is too dry.
Preheat oven to 180 °C and bake in greased patty pans or in paper cups for 10 minutes or until they are golden-brown. MAKES ABOUT 50

Treacle

Treacle gives any chocolate cake, dark cake or pudding a good colour and flavour.

625 ml (2½ cups) yellow sugar
about 250 ml (1 cup) water

HEAT A HEAVY-BASED pot on medium heat and add sugar, allowing it to burn. Do not stir.
When the sugar has melted completely, add a cup of water and stir until the sugar has changed colour to very dark brown.
Remove from heat and when cold, bottle in a wide-necked jar, seal well and store for further use. The treacle should be liquid enough to pour. MAKES ABOUT 500 ML

OPPOSITE   Zainab's Apple Tart, page 82

Aniseed Doughnuts

You can make these oval doughnuts the day before and the syrup just before serving.

15 g (1 tbsp) instant dry yeast
60 ml (1/4 cup) self-raising flour
750 ml (3 cups) cake flour
100 g (1/2 cup) butter
2 eggs, beaten
30 ml (2 tbsp) sugar
5 ml (1 tsp) aniseed
5 ml (1 tsp) salt
375 ml (11/2 cups) milk
375 ml (11/2 cups) oil

SYRUP
250 ml (1 cup) white sugar
10 ml (2 tsp) honey *or* golden syrup
250 ml (1 cup) warm water

MIX YEAST WITH a pinch of sugar and 10 ml (2 tsp) warm water and allow to stand for a few seconds until it froths.

Sift flours lightly, then rub in butter. Add remaining ingredients, except oil, to form a dough but do not knead. Cover with plastic or a table cloth and leave in a warm place for 11/2-2 hours or until doubled in size, then turn out onto a floured surface. Dip fingers into flour and stretch dough. Work with light movements and form into ovals.

Heat oil in a deep saucepan and fry doughnuts over medium heat for a few minutes until they have cracked slightly and are golden-brown.

To make the syrup, add sugar and honey or golden syrup to warm milk. Allow to boil until sugar has melted, then leave to cool completely. Prick each doughnut with a fork and, using a slotted spoon, sweep through syrup, drain and transfer to a platter. MAKES ABOUT 25

Koeksisters

These oblong koeksisters are often served in Malay homes on Sunday mornings. They can be deep-fried and frozen (without the syrup) for up to 14 days. Thaw for 1 hour, make the syrup and eat!

250 ml (1 cup) cake flour
250 ml (1 cup) self-raising flour
5 ml (1 tsp) salt
60 g (1/4 cup) butter
5 ml (1 tsp) ground ginger
5 ml (1 tsp) ground cinnamon
5 ml (1 tsp) ground mixed spice
2,5 ml (1/2 tsp) ground cardamom
10 ml (2 tsp) soft brown sugar
10 ml (2 tsp) white sugar
7,5 ml (11/2 tsp) instant dry yeast
375 ml (11/2 cups) warm water

SYRUP
250 ml (1 cup) water
125 ml (1/2 cup) sugar
15 ml (1 tbsp) desiccated coconut
1 piece of naartjie peel

IN A MIXING bowl, combine the flours with salt. Add butter and rub in lightly until it resembles fine breadcrumbs. Add remaining ingredients, using the warm water to form a dough. Do not knead. Cover with plastic and leave in a warm place for about 11/2-2 hours or until doubled in size, then turn out on a lightly floured surface.

Dip fingers and knife into flour and use your hands to stretch the dough. Cut into 4 cm x 8 cm strips and deep-fry over medium heat in a deep saucepan. Insert fork to check if done and remove quickly, one by one, and drain in a colander or on kitchen paper.

To make the syrup, bring water, sugar, coconut and naartjie peel to a slow boil in a large saucepan until syrup starts to bubble. Prick each koeksister, then lower into the syrup. Add as many koeksisters to the syrup as the pan will hold. Turn koeksisters and cook for 5 minutes each side or until browned. Remove from pan with a slotted spoon, placing them on a platter sprinkled with a little extra coconut. Sprinkle coconut over each layer of koeksisters and serve while hot with choice coffee. MAKES ABOUT 25

Jam Roll

A firm favourite in our community.

5 eggs, separated
250 ml (1 cup) castor sugar
5 ml (1 tsp) vanilla essence
a pinch fine salt
250 ml (1 cup) self-raising flour
10 ml (2 tsp) baking powder

FILLING
45 ml (3 tbsp) jam of your choice

BEAT EGG WHITES until slightly stiff and set aside. Beat yolks with sugar until creamy, then fold in whites and essence. Add dry ingredients and blend well to form a batter.

Spread dough on a greased Swiss roll tin and bake at 200 °C for 10 minutes. Turn out onto greaseproof paper sprinkled with castor sugar and carefully spread with jam. Quickly roll cake up inside greaseproof paper and let it soften for about 30 minutes. Remove greaseproof paper , cover with a cloth for a few minutes to sweat and cut into slices. MAKES 1 LOAF

NOTES

✔ The best place to leave dough to rise is in a warm bed! Place covered dough in mixing bowl on layers of newspaper on top of the blankets.

✔ Dried naartjie peel lasts indefinitely when stored in a jar. Dry it in the sun or in the oven at a temperature below 100 °C. Add naartjie peel to koeksisters, doughnuts, sweet potatoes or stewed mielies.

✔ It is better to use butter instead of margarine when baking sponge cakes.

Koeksisters, page 80

Date and Walnut Loaf

A favourite childhood recipe.

4 x 250 ml (4 cups) self-raising flour
500 ml (2 cups) cake flour
125 ml (½ cup) white sugar
125 ml (½ cup) soft brown sugar
15 ml (1 tbsp) oil
6 eggs
2,5 ml (½ tsp) vanilla essence
2 x 250 g packets dates rolled in
10 ml (2 tsp) flour
a pinch salt
500 ml (2 cups) walnuts
300 ml (1¼ cups) yellow sugar
15 ml (1 tbsp) water

COMBINE ALL INGREDIENTS, except yellow sugar and water, and set aside. Place yellow sugar in a dry pot on low heat and scorch until it is burnt. Remove from heat, add water, cover pot and leave to cool. Add to the rest of the ingredients and bake in a greased loaf tin at 140 °C for 1 hour. MAKES 1 LARGE LOAF

Crumbled Tart

Also called a German tart – serve on special occasions.

PASTRY
250 ml (1 cup) castor sugar
250 g (1 cup) butter
2 large or 3 medium eggs
15 ml (1 tbsp) oil
500 ml (2 cups) cake flour
500 ml (2 cups) self-raising flour

FILLING
625 ml (2½ cups) desiccated coconut
250 ml (1 cup) sugar
125 g (½ cup) apricot jam *or* jam of your choice

TO MAKE THE pastry, cream sugar and butter together, then add eggs, oil and flours to form a soft dough. Roll out and press into a greased baking sheet, leaving a little aside for grating over the top.
To make the filling, boil coconut and sugar until almost dry. Spread jam on pastry in baking sheet and cover with coconut mixture. Grate remaining pastry over and bake at 180 °C for about 30 minutes until light brown. Cool and cut into squares. MAKES ABOUT 10 SQUARES

N O T E S

✔ Apricot jam can be used to sandwich layer cakes together instead of icing. Or use any jam of your choice.
✔ Place a lemon in the cake tin and the cake will not dry out while storing.

Zainab's Apple Tart

This easy and mouth-watering recipe is guaranteed to satisfy the hungriest of friends! Make pastry as per the instructions for the Milk Tart, below.

FILLING
5 cooking apples, peeled, cored and
thickly wedged
1 clove
10 ml (2 tsp) golden syrup (optional)
a pinch ground cinnamon
15 ml (1 tbsp) soft brown sugar
60 ml (¼ cup) water
handful seedless raisins (optional)

SIMMER APPLES, CLOVE, golden syrup if using, cinnamon, sugar and water until soft and brown. The mixture must be syrupy rather than liquid. Set aside to cool.

Roll out the pastry on a floured surface and line a greased pie dish with it, keeping a little of the pastry aside for the topping.

Spread apple mixture onto pastry, scatter over raisins if using, and grate or crumble remaining pastry over.

Bake at 180 °C for 30 minutes or until golden-brown. SERVES 8

Milk Tart

Serve with tea and you won't need a meal!

PASTRY
125 g (½ cup) butter
250 ml (¾ cup) castor sugar
5 ml (1 tsp) vanilla essence
1 egg, beaten
250 ml (1 cup) cake flour
250 ml (1 cup) self-raising flour
10 ml (2 tsp) oil
a pinch salt

FILLING
1 litre (4 cups) milk
10 large eggs
310 ml (1¼ cups) sugar
15 ml (1 tbsp) cake flour, made into
a paste with 30 ml (2 tbsp) water
2,5 ml (½ tsp) ground cardamom

TO MAKE THE pastry, cream butter and sugar together, then add vanilla essence. Add egg, then gradually add the flours, oil and salt and work lightly to form a soft and pliable dough. Set aside.

To make the filling, slowly bring milk to the boil. Meanwhile, beat eggs and sugar together. Remove milk from heat and pour slowly into egg and sugar mixture. Continue stirring, then add flour paste and set aside.

Grease a heavy-based ovenproof dish lightly with butter. Roll out pastry on a floured surface and line dish with it. Pour in filling, place small nuts of butter on top, sprinkle with ground cardamom and bake on bottom shelf of oven at 200 °C for 40 minutes. SERVES 10

Cardamom Sandwich Cake

The ground cardamom gives this cake an interesting flavour.

125 g (½ cup) soft butter
375 ml (1½ cups) castor sugar
3 eggs, separated
7,5 ml (1½ tsp) ground cardamom
4 x 250 ml (4 cups) self-raising flour
a pinch of salt
5 ml (1 tsp) baking powder
250 ml (½ cup) milk *or* water
60 ml (¼ cup) oil

CREAM BUTTER AND sugar together until smooth, then add egg yolks and cardamom, stirring in one direction only to prevent holes forming in the mixture. Now add flour, salt, baking powder and milk or water. Beat egg whites until stiff and fold in, then add oil, mixing well.

Pour into a greased bread pan and bake at 180 °C on middle shelf for 1 hour. Remove from oven and leave to cool in tins before removing to wire rack. Cover in a cloth and allow to sweat for about 5 minutes. MAKES 1 LOAF

Orange Layer Cake

Simply delicious served with a cup of tea. Instead of using icing to sandwich the cakes together, use apricot jam.

125 g (½ cup) soft butter
185 ml (¾ cup) castor sugar
a pinch salt
3 large eggs, separated
juice of 1 large orange
2 drops orange essence
15 ml (1 tbsp) oil
10 ml (2 tsp) grated orange rind
125 ml (½ cup) milk
750 ml (3 cups) cake flour
15 ml (1 tbsp) baking powder

ICING
345 ml (1⅓ cup) icing sugar
60 ml (¼ cup) orange juice
30 ml (2 tbsp) melted butter
60 ml (¼ cup) boiling water

CREAM BUTTER, SUGAR and salt together. Add egg yolks, orange juice, essence, oil, rind and milk, mixing well.

Beat egg whites until stiff and fold into batter. Blend well, then add flour and baking powder, stirring in one direction only.

Grease two round baking tins with oil. Sprinkle 5 ml (1 tsp) flour into each tin and pour equal amounts of batter into each tin. Bake at 180 °C on middle shelf for 20-25 minutes. Remove from oven and allow to sweat first by covering with a cloth. When quite cold, remove from tins.

To make the icing, mix all the ingredients together ensuring that icing is not too runny. Fill and ice cake by dipping flat knife or palette in cold water to spread icing more easily, shaking off excess water from knife. Decorate as desired. MAKES 1 CAKE

Rich Chocolate Cake
A bitter-sweet wonder cake!

1 x 125 g tin cocoa
30 ml (2 tbsp) sugar
60 ml (¼ cup) milk
60 ml (¼ cup) water
3 large eggs, separated
125 g (½ cup) soft butter
375 ml (1½ cups) castor sugar
a pinch salt
750 ml (3 cups) cake flour
15 ml (1 tbsp) baking powder
10 ml (2 tsp) treacle (*see* page 78)
15 ml (1 tbsp) oil

ICING
60 ml (¼ cup) warm water
240 g (1¾ cups) icing sugar
80 g (⅓ cup) butter

OVER LOW HEAT, cook a little more than half the tin of cocoa with the sugar, milk and water. Stir to prevent mixture from sticking to the bottom of the saucepan. Drops of cold water can be added if it is too sticky. Set aside to cool.

Beat egg whites until stiff and set aside. Cream butter and castor sugar with salt until smooth. Add egg yolks, blending well. Stir into cold chocolate mixture. Sift flour and baking powder and stir into mixture – do not beat, but blend well. Fold in egg whites, add treacle and oil, and mix thoroughly.

Pour cake batter into two greased round layer cake tins. Bake at 180 °C for 20 minutes. Remove from oven. Loosen cakes with a thin-blade knife and leave in tins to sweat under a cloth for a few minutes. Turn out onto a wire rack and cover with a dry cloth to prevent drying out.

To make the icing, add small amounts of the warm water to the icing sugar, about 60 ml (¼ cup) cocoa (use more cocoa for a more bitter icing) and butter. Ice the cakes and decorate if desired with chocolate twirls or coconut. MAKES 1 CAKE

Milk Tart, page 82

Pineapple Tart
Use the Puff Pastry recipe to make this.

FILLING
1 pineapple, peeled and coarsely grated
60 ml (¼ cup) sugar
250 ml (1 cup) water
1 piece stick cinnamon

TOPPING
60 ml (¼ cup) desiccated coconut
30 ml (2 tbsp) sugar

MAKE THE PASTRY according to the Puff Pastry recipe on page 78.

To make the filling, cook pineapple, sugar, water and cinnamon for 15 minutes over low heat until almost dry. If pineapple is watery, cook for a little longer. Set aside to cool.

To make the topping, cook the coconut and sugar together until semi-dry, about 15 minutes. When everything has cooled completely, roll out pastry and line tart plates or ordinary porcelain plates, saving some for decorating. Spread filling into tart shells, add topping, cut remaining pastry into strips and make a criss-cross pattern over topping. Bake at 200 °C for 5 minutes on the bottom shelf, then transfer to the middle shelf and bake for a further 15 minutes.
MAKES 2 TARTS

Flan Tarts
Use flan baking tins for these tarts.

FLAN
45 ml (3 tbsp) water
45 ml (3 tbsp) milk
125 g (½ cup) butter
250 ml (1 cup) sugar
3 eggs
4 x 250 ml (4 cups) flour
10 ml (2 tsp) baking powder

FILLING
1 pineapple, peeled and grated
15 ml (1 tbsp) sugar
15 ml (1 tbsp) custard powder
5 ml (1 tsp) butter, melted
1 egg yolk
a little milk
cherry halves for decoration

TO MAKE THE flans, boil together water, milk and butter. Allow to cool. Add sugar and beat. Add remaining ingredients to form a cake batter. Bake at 180 °C in two flan baking tins for 20-25 minutes.

To make the filling, boil the pineapple with the sugar. Make a paste with the custard, butter, egg yolk and a little milk. Stir into the pineapple mixture and boil for 3 minutes. Allow to cool before pouring into flan cases.

Decorate with the cherry halves.
MAKES 2 FLANS

Cream Cracker Tart
My famous Sunday family tart!

CRUST
250 ml (1 cup) cream crackers, crumbled
30 ml (2 tbsp) melted butter
30 ml (2 tbsp) sugar
a pinch ground cinnamon

FILLING
30 ml (2 tbsp) cornflour
2 eggs, separated
250 ml (1 cup) milk
nely ground cinnamon for decoration

MIX CRUMBS, BUTTER, sugar and innamon together to form a crust. ress onto base of a greased oven-roof pie dish.

To make the filling, blend cornflour and egg yolks with milk to form a custard. Bring to the boil until thickened. Cool and pour into crust in pie dish. Whip egg whites until stiff and spread over custard. Bake at 180 °C for 30 minutes. Sprinkle with ground cinnamon after baking. MAKES 1 TART

Coffee Loaf
A tea time loaf, delicious with cheese.

200 g (1⅓ cups) seedless raisins
80 ml (⅓ cup) soft brown sugar
560 ml (2¼ cups) hot, strong liquid coffee
4 x 250 ml (4 cups) self-raising flour
2,5 ml (¼ tsp) ground ginger
60 ml (¼ cup) oil
2,5 ml (½ tsp) salt
5 ml (1 tsp) aniseed
1 egg, beaten
30 ml (2 tbsp) butter, melted

ABOVE   Rich Chocolate Cake, page 83

PREHEAT OVEN TO 180 °C. Soak raisins and sugar in the hot coffee for 5 minutes and allow to cool.

In a mixing bowl, sift flour, add the remaining ingredients, including raisins and sugar, stirring with a wooden spoon. Bake in a well-greased loaf tin for 30-40 minutes. Place on a wire rack, cover with a cloth and leave to sweat for a few minutes before serving. MAKES 1 LOAF

N O T E S

✔ When baking biscuits or pastry, first bake on the second shelf of the oven for 5 minutes, then transfer to the middle shelf for further baking.

✔ A few drops of lemon juice added to icing gives it a good flavour and colouring.

Corn Flake Biscuits

These ingredients will be in your pantry.

125 g (½ cup) soft butter
125 ml (½ cup) soft brown sugar
2 eggs, beaten
4 x 250 ml (4 cups) corn flakes
2,5 ml (½ tsp) salt
10 ml (2 tsp) oil
375 ml (1½ cups) self-raising flour
2,5 ml (½ tsp) vanilla essence
6 dates, chopped
10 walnuts, quartered

CREAM BUTTER AND sugar together. Add eggs, then remaining ingredients, working together by hand. Roll out dough, not too thinly. Cut out shapes with a cookie cutter and place on a greased baking sheet. Bake at 180 °C on bottom shelf of oven for 7 minutes, then on middle shelf for 10 minutes. Cool on a wire rack. MAKES 36

Saboeratjies

These traditional biscuits are always decorated with three currants.

4 x 250 ml (4 cups) cake flour
5 ml (1 tsp) baking powder
2 eggs, beaten
200 ml (1 cup) caramel *or* soft brown sugar
250 g (1 cup) butter
12 cardamom pods, pounded
5 ml (1 tsp) ground ginger
5 ml (1 tsp) mixed spice
125 ml (½ cup) oil
125 ml (½ cup) currants

COMBINE ALL INGREDIENTS, except currants, to form a dough. Roll out dough. Cut out with oblong cookie cutter and place on a greased baking tray. Press three currants in a row down the centre of each cookie. Bake at 180 °C on second shelf of oven for 5 minutes, then on middle shelf for 7 minutes until golden-brown. MAKES ABOUT 40

Crunchy Oat and Nut Biscuits

Dates are often used in Malay cooking – I'm especially fond of baking with them.

125 g (½ cup) butter
250 ml (1 cup) brown sugar
2 eggs, beaten
60 ml (¼ cup) oil
375 ml (1½ cups) self-raising flour
60 g (¼ cup) fine oats
750 ml (3 cups) corn flakes
2 Weet-Bix, crushed
2,5 ml (½ tsp) caramel essence
20 pecan nuts, quartered
½ x 250 g packet dates, chopped
10 ml (2 tsp) ground ginger

CREAM BUTTER AND sugar together. Add eggs, then remaining ingredients. Mix well and form into balls the size of a large marble. Place on a greased baking tray and flatten slightly with a fork. Bake at 180 °C on second shelf of oven for 6 minutes, then on middle shelf for a further 10 minutes. MAKES ABOUT 60

Pronutro and Wholemeal Biscuits

250 ml (1 cup) wholemeal flour
200 g (1 cup) brown sugar
125 ml (½ cup) wheat germ
250 ml (1 cup) Pronutro
125 ml (½ cup) desiccated coconut
125 g (½ cup) soft butter
a pinch salt
2 eggs, beaten
15 ml (1 tbsp) oil

MIX DRY INGREDIENTS together, then add remaining ingredients and blend well to form a dough. Roll out dough on floured surface and cut into thin sausage shapes about 1,5 cm in width and 5 cm long. Place on a greased baking tray and press lightly with a fork. Bake at 180 °C on middle shelf for 12 minutes. MAKES ABOUT 60

Soetkoekies

Red bole is available in powder form from pharmacies.

75 g (5 tbsp) butter
75 ml (5 tbsp) oil
400 ml (1½ cups) yellow sugar
5 ml (1 tsp) mixed spice
2,5 ml (½ tsp) ground nutmeg
5 ml (1 tsp) ground cinnamon
2,5 ml (½ tsp) ground cardamom
3 whole cloves, pounded
2 eggs, beaten
4 x 250 ml (4 cups) cake flour
2,5 ml (½ tsp) bicarbonate of soda
5 ml (1 tsp) red bole

CREAM BUTTER, OIL and sugar together until soft. Stir in spices and eggs, mixing well. Sift flour and bicarbonate of soda together and add, stirring in a little milk if the dough is too dry.
 Mix red bole with a third of the dough. Roll out the remaining two-thirds on a floured surface and dot with pieces of the red bole dough. Roll out to ½ cm thick and cut out heart-shaped biscuits with a cutter. Press half a peanut in the centre of each biscuit if desired. Place on a greased baking tray and bake at 200 °C for 5 minutes on the bottom shelf and for a further 10 minutes on the middle shelf. MAKES 50-60

Karamonk Scraps

This is an old recipe for cardamom biscuits, a Malay speciality. If desired, press a tiny pink scented sweet in the middle of each biscuit before baking.

2 eggs
470 ml (2 cups) sugar
125 g (½ cup) butter
4 x 250 ml (4 cups) cake flour
15 ml (1 tbsp) oil
5 ml (1 tsp) baking powder
2,5 ml (½ tsp) rose water
3 cardamom pods, pounded *or*
5 ml (1 tsp) ground cardamom

CREAM EGGS AND sugar together well and set aside. Rub butter into flour and then mix in remaining ingredients, including the egg and sugar mixture, lightly to form a soft dough. Roll out to 1 cm thickness. Using cookie cutters, cut into shapes and bake at 180 °C, first on bottom shelf for 6 minutes and then on top shelf for a further 6 minutes. Enjoy when cool. MAKES ABOUT 60

N O T E

✔ Pound cardamom pods with a hammer between two pieces of greaseproof paper.

BELOW   Butter Biscuits, Karamonk Scraps, Saboeratjies and Crunchy Oat and Nut Biscuits, pages 86 & 87

Butter Biscuits

250 g (1 cup) soft butter
7,5 ml (1½ tsp) oil
500 ml (2 cups) yellow sugar
2,5 ml (½ tsp) vanilla essence
1 large egg, beaten
4 x 250 ml (4 cups) cake flour
2,5 ml (½ tsp) bicarbonate of soda

CREAM BUTTER, OIL and sugar together until light, then add essence and egg. Add flour and bicarbonate of soda and mix together to form a fairly stiff dough. Roll out dough on a floured surface and cut out diamond shapes with a cookie cutter. Decorate with pieces of angelica and cherry. Place on a greased baking tray and bake at 200 °C for 10 minutes. Cool on wire racks. MAKES 50

Ginger Nuts
These should be slightly sticky when baked.

115 g (½ cup) butter
145 ml (½ cup) soft brown sugar
10 ml (2 tsp) golden syrup
juice of ½ lemon *or* 15 ml (1 tsp) bottled lemon juice
250 ml (1 cup) cake flour
2,5 ml (½ tsp) baking powder
10 ml (2 tsp) ground ginger

MELT BUTTER AND sugar in a saucepan with syrup and lemon juice, stirring slowly. Remove from heat and add flour, baking powder and ginger. Mix well to form a dough. Place teaspoonfuls of dough on a baking tray lined with well-greased paper. Bake at 200 °C for 10-12 minutes. MAKES ABOUT 20

Breads and Fritters

Many of these bread recipes are my own creations, tried and tested over the years. I've also included recipes for rotis and pizza dough here. Fritters, with a variety of fillings, are also called 'vetkoekies' and are often served after dinner.

Nutty Wheat Brown Bread

The queen of brown breads and simple too.

125 ml (½ cup) wheat germ
60 ml (¼ cup) digestive bran
4 x 250 ml (4 cups) Nutty Wheat Flour
5 ml (1 tsp) medium-coarse salt
2,5 ml (½ tsp) bicarbonate of soda
30 ml (2 tbsp) honey *or* golden syrup
500 ml (2 cups) stirred Bulgarian
yoghurt *or* buttermilk
250 ml (1 cup) sesame seeds
1 egg, beaten
15 ml (1 tbsp) oil
125 ml (½ cup) milk
7,5 ml (1½ tsp) salt

PREHEAT OVEN TO 180 °C. Mix all ingredients together to form a dough. Place dough in a well-greased baking tin and bake on the middle shelf for about 1 hour and 10 minutes. Use a skewer to test if bread is ready – if the skewer comes out clean, the bread is ready. Place on wire rack to cool, cover with a cloth and leave to sweat for a few minutes. MAKES 1 LOAF

Special Milk Loaves

8 x 250 ml (8 cups) cake flour
500 ml (2 cups) self-raising flour
500 ml (2 cups) milk
250 ml (1 cup) water
30 ml (2 tbsp) sugar
7,5 ml (1 ½ tsp) salt
15 g (1 tbsp) instant dry yeast
2 eggs, beaten

SIFT FLOURS IN a mixing bowl. Heat milk and water together until warm but not too hot, remove from stove and add sugar, salt and yeast. Pour most of the milk mixture into the flour and knead to form a dough. Add beaten eggs and rest of the milk mixture, working dough with your hands for 5 minutes. Cover dough completely with plastic and leave to rise for about 2 hours. Turn out onto a floured surface and cut into 3 pieces.

Working lightly, punch down and place in three greased baking tins to prove for 30 minutes. Bake on middle shelf at 200 °C for 40 minutes.

Remove from oven, cover with a cloth and allow to sweat for a few seconds. Turn out onto a wire rack and gloss the tops and sides with butter. Wrap in cloths and leave to sweat in an upright position to let the steam escape. MAKES 2 LARGE LOAVES AND 1 SMALL LOAF

OPPOSITE   Quick Onion Bread (left), page 90, and Sunflower and Sesame Seed Loaf (right), page 91

Mosbrood

Grape bread is a treat from the old days and must be made in summer when grapes are in season.

1 kg hanepoot grapes, peeled and pitted
125 g (1/2 cup) butter *or* margarine
60 ml (1/4 cup) oil
10 x 250 ml (10 cups) white bread flour
4 x 250 ml (4 cups) self-raising flour
60 ml (1/4 cup) white sugar
10 ml (2 tsp) aniseed
10 ml (2 tsp) medium-coarse salt
1 egg, beaten
10 ml (2 tsp) instant dry yeast

PLACE GRAPES IN a large bowl and mash roughly to form a pulp. Cover bowl with plastic and leave to stand overnight. Heat the pulp slowly in a pot until lukewarm before using.

Place grape pulp, butter and oil in a mixing bowl. Combine all dry ingredients, add to bowl and knead to form a dough. Allow to rise for 2 hours, then punch down very lightly. Turn out onto a floured surface and divide dough in half. Place in 2 well-greased baking pans.

Preheat oven to 200 °C and bake on middle shelf for 40 minutes. Remove loaves from the oven, gloss top and sides with a little butter or margarine and wrap in dry cloths to sweat for a few minutes.

Serve with your favourite jam and filter coffee. MAKES 2 LOAVES

Light Brown Rolls

Ideal for a picnic or with a salad.

500 ml (2 cups) white cake flour
250 ml (1 cup) brown bread meal
250 ml (1 cup) self-raising flour
10 ml (2 tsp) instant dry yeast
15 ml (1 tbsp) butter
2,5 ml (1/2 tsp) medium-coarse salt
10 ml (2 tsp) oil
375 ml (1 1/2 cups) warm water
1 egg, beaten

SIFT DRY INGREDIENTS together in a large bowl. Add remaining ingredients and knead to form a dough. Turn out onto a floured surface and form dough into a sausage shape. Cut 2 cm lengths off with a knife, roll into balls and place, slightly apart, on a well-greased baking tray.

Preheat oven to 180 °C. Cover the baking tray with plastic and leave dough to rise and double in size for 30 minutes. Remove plastic and bake on the middle shelf of the oven for 25 minutes. Remove rolls from oven and gloss tops with a little butter. Wrap in cloths and leave to sweat for a few minutes. MAKES 24 ROLLS

Mosbolletjies

Mosbolletjies or aniseed balls are delicious served with white cheese and coffee. Bits of orange or lemon peel can be added to the dough.

125 g (1/2 cup) butter
4 x 250 ml (4 cups) self-raising flour
125 ml (1/2 cup) cake flour
2 eggs, beaten
10 g (2 tsp) yeast diluted with
2,5 ml (1/2 tsp) sugar and
15 ml (1 tbsp) lukewarm water
5 ml (1 tsp) aniseed
30 ml (2 tbsp) castor sugar
2,5 ml (1/2 tsp) salt
185 ml (3/4 cup) warm milk
10 ml (2 tsp) oil

RUB BUTTER LIGHTLY into sifted flours using your fingers and then add eggs. Add diluted yeast, aniseed, sugar, salt, milk and oil and blend lightly – do not knead. The dough must be loose, soft and moist.

Break dough into balls of a similar size to scones, place on a greased baking sheet and bake for 20 minutes at 180 °C or until golden-brown. Turn out onto a wire rack and brush with sugar water. Cover with a cloth and leave to sweat for a few minutes. MAKES 12-14 BALLS

Cheese and Parsley Bread

My granny used to make this round, savoury loaf – treat your family to it.

750 ml (3 cups) cake flour
125 ml (1/2 cup) self-raising flour
7,5 ml (1 1/2 tsp) medium-coarse salt
10 g (2 tsp) instant dry yeast
10 ml (2 tsp) sugar
30 ml (2 tbsp) melted butter
100 g (1/2 cup) grated Parmesan *or* Cheddar cheese
1 large egg, beaten
60 ml (1/4 cup) chopped parsley
375 ml (1 1/2 cups) warm milk

COMBINE ALL DRY ingredients in a large mixing bowl. Add remaining ingredients to form a dough and knead well, working lightly. Leave to rise until double in size, then punch down and turn out onto a floured surface. Make a round loaf and transfer it to a well-greased, deep, round baking pan. Oil a piece of plastic, cover the pan and leave to stand in a warm spot for about 30 minutes.

Preheat oven to 200 °C. Remove the plastic and bake bread on middle shelf for 30 minutes, then turn out onto a wire rack and gloss top and sides with a little butter or margarine. Wrap in a cloth and leave to sweat for a few minutes – the cloth helps to keep the crust soft. MAKES 1 LOAF

Quick Onion Bread

This loaf won't last long – your family will polish it off in no time!

2 eggs, beaten
30 ml (2 tbsp) condensed milk
15 ml (1 tbsp) oil
5 x 250 ml (5 cups) cake flour
20 ml (1 1/2 tbsp) self-raising flour
15 g (1 tbsp) instant dry yeast
7,5 ml (1 1/2 tsp) medium-coarse salt
125 ml (1/2 cup) onion slices, fried in 10 ml (2 tsp) oil
375 ml (1 1/2 cups) boiling water

COMBINE EGGS, CONDENSED milk and oil, mix well and set aside.

Mix flours, yeast and salt together. Add fried onions, water, slightly cooled, and the egg and condensed milk mixture. Make into a dough using your fingers and the heel of your hands. Transfer dough to a greased bread pan and place in an airtight plastic bag. Cover with a cloth and leave in a warm place for about 25-30 minutes.

Preheat oven to 200 °C. Remove dough from plastic bag and bake bread on the middle shelf of the oven for 40 minutes – the bread will rise quickly. Remove from oven and allow to stand for 2 minutes. Turn out and gloss the sides and top of the loaf with a little butter or margarine. Wrap in a cloth and leave to sweat – this will ensure a soft crust. MAKES 2 MEDIUM LOAVES, OR 1 LARGE AND 1 SMALL LOAF

Sunflower and Sesame Seed Loaf
A sure winner!

4 x 250 ml (4 cups) Nutty Wheat Flour
60 ml (¼ cup) digestive bran
60 ml (¼ cup) self-raising flour
5 ml (1 tsp) bicarbonate of soda
5 ml (1 tsp) medium-coarse salt
60 ml (¼ cup) sesame seeds
60 ml (¼ cup) sunflower seeds
500 ml (2 cups) stirred Bulgarian yoghurt
10 ml (2 tsp) treacle (*see* page 78)
30 ml (2 tbsp) honey *or* golden syrup
1 egg, beaten, mixed with 125 ml (½ cup) milk and 15 ml (1 tbsp) oil

IN A LARGE mixing bowl, mix dry ingredients together with a wooden spoon and then add yoghurt. Blend well, then add treacle and honey and milk mixture, mixing thoroughly.

Grease a sandwich loaf baking pan and line the bottom with greaseproof paper. Pour mixture into pan, cover with plastic and leave to prove for about 10 minutes.

Preheat oven to 180 °C. Remove plastic and bake on middle shelf of oven for about 1 hour.

Remove from pan, gloss top and sides with a little soft butter or margarine, wrap in a cloth and leave to sweat standing in a vertical position – this lets the steam escape from under the bread. MAKES 1 LOAF

> **N O T E**
>
> ✔ Line bread pans with greaseproof paper or brown paper. To aid the bread rising, wrap in an airtight plastic bag and a thick cloth.

BELOW   Mosbolletjies, page 90

Malay Roti

Roti is the Malay word for unleavened bread, adapted from the Indian recipe, and is often served with curries instead of rice. Use your fingers to break off a piece of roti and scoop up some curry.

750 ml (3 cups) cake flour
a pinch baking powder
7,5 ml (1½ tsp) medium-coarse salt
375 ml (1½ cups) warm water
75 g (5 tbsp) butter, melted
125 ml (½ cup) oil

MIX FLOUR, BAKING powder, salt and water together to form a dough. On a floured surface, work dough until pliable, bringing it together with your fingers. Add a little oil if necessary to make working the dough easier. Roll out and smear with the melted butter. Sprinkle with a little flour and roll up to form a long, thick sausage. Cut it into 5 cm long pieces and stand pieces on their sides, so that the whirls are visible.

Roll and turn each piece of dough a few times to form a rough circle, about 20 cm in diameter and as thick as a pancake – it must not be too thin. Cut off any sharp edges with a sharp knife to make it round.

Heat a cast-iron pan or heavy-based pan over medium heat and smear with a little oil, about 5 ml (1 tsp). Place a roti in the pan and dab with oil using hard greaseproof paper or butter paper. As it cooks, the roti will rise and bubble slightly. Turn with a palette or an egg lifter about four times until it is lightly browned and speckled on both sides.

Take freshly cooked roti and crunch gently in your hands to give it a crumpled effect. Transfer to a fairly deep dish and cover with a cloth to allow the roti to sweat – this prevents the edges becoming rough. Continue making rotis until all the dough has been used. If there's a tendency to dryness while frying, dab a little more oil on the roti. MAKES ABOUT 7

NOTES

✔ Using boiling water instead of warm water will give you a flat roti, similar to pita bread. The warm water makes it flaky.

✔ TO FREEZE: Layer cooked rotis with greaseproof paper between them. Wrap in foil so that they are airtight, and freeze. Defrost by warming them slowly in a 100 °C oven, steam, covered, over a pot of boiling water, or microwave on 50% for 20-30 seconds per roti.

✔ For good results, chill your rolling pin in the fridge before using it.

Rice Fritters

500 ml (2 cups) cooked rice
a pinch ground nutmeg
1 egg, beaten
10 ml (2 tsp) butter, melted
250 ml (1 cup) cake flour
5 ml (1 tsp) baking powder
milk to bind
375 ml (1½ cups) oil
cinnamon sugar for dusting

BLEND ALL INGREDIENTS together,
except oil and cinnamon sugar, to
form a stiffish batter, which must
be neither too dry nor too wet.

Heat oil in a deep pan on medium-
high. Dip a tablespoon into the oil
and then into the batter; fry spoonfuls until golden-brown on both sides.
Lift out with an egg lifter; drain on
greaseproof paper. Sprinkle with cinnamon sugar. MAKES ABOUT 20 SMALL
OR 14 LARGE FRITTERS

Pumpkin Fritters

*Also called 'pampoen vetkoekies', they
are favourite tea time and TV treats
in our family.*

500 g pumpkin, peeled, cooked,
drained and pulped
250 ml (1 cup) cake flour
5 ml (1 tsp) baking powder
1 egg, beaten
a pinch salt
30 ml (2 tbsp) melted butter
a pinch ground nutmeg
60 ml (¼ cup) milk
375 ml (1½ cups) oil
cinnamon sugar for dusting

MIX ALL INGREDIENTS together,
except oil and cinnamon sugar, to
form a stiffish batter.

Heat oil in heavy-based frying pan
on medium-high, using only enough
to generously cover the bottom of the
pan. Dip a dessertspoon into the
oil, then into the batter, and drop
spoonfuls of batter into the pan. Fry
until golden-brown on both sides. Lift
out with a slotted spoon or an egg
lifter and drain on greaseproof paper
or brown paper.

Serve hot, dusted with cinnamon
sugar. MAKES ABOUT 20 SMALL OR
14 LARGE FRITTERS

N O T E S

✔ 500 g potatoes, mashed with a dash of
milk, can be used instead of pumpkin for
the Pumpkin Fritters.
✔ For a delicious variation, substitute
well-drained whole-kernel corn for rice in
the Rice Fritters.
✔ Never peel an orange with a knife.
Rather, toss it in boiling water and leave
for 10 minutes, then peel it by hand. It
makes the orange easier to peel and it
won't be bitter.

Potato Fritters

Use 500 g peeled sweet potatoes instead of potatoes, if preferred. Cut them into chips which will stick out of the fritters when cooked, giving them an uneven shape.

2 large potatoes, peeled and halved
60 g (¼ cup) butter, melted
250 ml (1 cup) cake flour
2,5 ml (½ tsp) baking powder
1 egg, beaten
a pinch ground nutmeg
60 ml (¼ cup) cold milk
250 ml (1 cup) oil
cinnamon sugar for dusting

COOK POTATOES AND mash with butter. Add remaining ingredients, except oil and cinnamon sugar, to form a pliable batter.

Heat oil in a large, shallow pan – there must be enough oil to generously cover the bottom on the pan. Dip a dessertspoon into the hot oil, then into the batter, and drop spoonfuls of batter into the oil. Fry until golden-brown. Remove with a slotted spoon, roll in cinnamon sugar and serve hot. MAKES ABOUT 20 SMALL OR 14 LARGE FRITTERS

Pizza

Remember to always have peeled and pulped tomatoes as your first layer on the pizza base. See the Notes (this page) for filling suggestions.

DOUGH
1 egg, beaten
2,5 ml (½ tsp) salt
500 ml (2 cups) flour
7,5 ml (1½ tsp) baking powder
125 ml (½ cup) warm milk
5 ml (1 tsp) sugar
5 ml (1 tsp) oil
2,5 ml (½ tsp) chilli powder
a pinch dried tarragon
a pinch dried oregano
a pinch dried thyme
5 ml (1 tsp) masala

TO MAKE THE dough, mix all ingredients together, except masala, in a mixing bowl, working until soft and pliable. Roll out dough on a floured surface and sprinkle with masala. Grease a pizza pan and line with dough. Bake blind at 180 °C for 5 minutes on middle shelf. Remove from oven. Top it with a filling of your choice.

It's best eaten immediately but can be heated in the oven later. MAKES 1 MEDIUM PIZZA

N O T E S

✔ Various fillings can be used – first spread a layer of tomatoe pulp over the base, then add your filling and sprinkle grated cheese over if desired. Bake at 180 °C for 20 minutes or until cheese has melted.
✔ Tangy pilchard or tuna smoor, flaked chicken cooked with mushrooms and herbs, shrimp and mussel smoor, or fried mince seasoned with herbs and cooked with onion, mushroom and tomato and a little masala are some of the fillings that may tempt you.

Pumpkin Puffs

In winter we eat these nearly every night with a hot drink.

250 ml (1 cup) cake flour
125 ml (½ cup) self-raising flour
5 ml (1 tsp) salt
5 ml (1 tsp) baking powder
30 ml (2 tbsp) butter *or* margarine
500 g pumpkin, cooked, drained and pulped
1 egg, beaten
30 ml (2 tbsp) currants
a pinch ground nutmeg
375 ml (1½ cups) oil
cinnamon sugar for dusting

SIFT FLOURS, SALT and baking powder together. Add remaining ingredients, except oil and cinnamon sugar, and gently mix. The mixture should not be too runny. If the mixture is too dry, add a little cold milk.

Heat oil in small saucepan on low heat. Using a long-handled spoon, dip into oil first, then into the batter and drop spoonfuls of batter into the oil. Fry a few puffs at a time so that they don't stick together – they sometimes turn on their own. Keep heat on low or the puffs will burn on the outside and remain raw in the centre. To test if they are done, pierce with a fork – if the fork is dry, the puffs are ready. Remove from pan with a slotted spoon and allow to drain on absorbent paper. Dust with cinnamon sugar and serve immediately while still hot. MAKES ABOUT 20 SMALL OR 15 BIG PUFFS

Sweetcorn Puffs

Another tasty after-dinner or TV snack to serve with coffee.

125 ml (½ cup) cake flour
250 ml (1 cup) self-raising flour
250 ml (1 cup) milk
1 x 410 g tin whole-kernel corn, drained
1 drop butter essence
2,5 ml (½ tsp) salt
30 ml (2 tbsp) butter *or* margarine, melted
1 egg, beaten
5 ml (1 tsp) baking powder
375 ml (1½ cups) oil
cinnamon sugar for dusting

SIFT FLOURS TOGETHER and add milk slowly to form a batter. Mix in remaining ingredients, except oil and cinnamon sugar.

Heat oil on medium-high. Dip a tablespoon first into the oil, then into the batter, and drop spoonfuls of batter into the oil. Flip over, then pierce with fork – a dry fork indicates the puffs are done. Remove with a slotted spoon and drain on greaseproof or brown paper.

Roll in cinnamon sugar and serve hot with a choice coffee. MAKES ABOUT 20 SMALL OR 15 LARGE PUFFS

Pumpkin Fritters, page 93, and Sweetcorn Puffs, page 94

Index